Milton's Sonnets

A. W. Verity

Alpha Editions

This edition published in 2020

ISBN : 9789354188732 (Hardback)

ISBN : 9789354188091 (Paperback)

Design and Setting By
Alpha Editions
www.alphaedis.com
email - alphaedis@gmail.com

As per information held with us this book is in Public Domain.
This book is a reproduction of an important historical work. Alpha Editions uses the best technology to reproduce historical work in the same manner it was first published to preserve its original nature. Any marks or number seen are left intentionally to preserve its true form.

NOTE.

THE sketch of Milton's life is inserted in this volume as it illustrates some points that occur in the Sonnets.

A. W. V.

April, 1895.

CONTENTS.

	PAGES
INTRODUCTION	ix—xxxii
LIFE OF MILTON	ix—xxiii
INTRODUCTION TO THE SONNETS . . .	xxiv—xxviii
A SELECTION OF CRITICISMS ON THE SONNETS	xxix—xxxii
SONNETS	1—27
NOTES	29—63
GLOSSARY	64—66
APPENDIX	67—76
INDEXES	77—78

INTRODUCTION.

LIFE OF MILTON.

MILTON'S life falls into three clearly defined divisions. The first period ends with the poet's return from Italy in 1639; the second at the Restoration in 1660, when release from the fetters of politics enabled him to remind the world that he was a great poet, if not a great controversialist; the third is brought to a close with his death in 1674. *Paradise Lost* belongs to the last of these periods; but we propose to summarise briefly the main events of all three. *The three periods in Milton's life.*

John Milton was born on December 9, 1608, in London. He came, in his own words, *ex genere honesto*. A family of Miltons had been settled in Oxfordshire since the reign of Elizabeth. The poet's father had been educated at an Oxford school, possibly as a chorister in one of the College choir-schools, and imbibing Anglican sympathies had conformed to the Established Church. For this he was disinherited by his father. He settled in London, following the profession of scrivener. A scrivener combined the occupations of lawyer and law-stationer. It appears to have been a lucrative calling; certainly John Milton (the poet was named after the father) attained to easy circumstances. He married about 1600, and had six children, of whom several died young. The third child was the poet. *Born 1608; the poet's father.*

The elder Milton was evidently a man of considerable culture, in particular an accomplished musician, and a composer[1] whose madrigals were deemed worthy of being printed side by side with those of Byrd, Orlando Gibbons and other leading musicians of the time. To him, no doubt, the poet owed the love of music of which we see frequent indications in the poems[2]. Realising, too, that in his son lay the promise and possibility of future greatness, John Milton took the utmost pains to have the boy adequately educated; and the lines *Ad Patrem* show that the ties of affection between father and child were of more than ordinary closeness.

Milton was sent to St Paul's School as a day scholar about the year 1620. He also had a tutor, Thomas Young, a Scotchman, who subsequently became Master of Jesus College, Cambridge. More important still, Milton grew up in the stimulating atmosphere of cultured home-life. This was a signal advantage. There are few who realise that the word 'culture' signifies anything very definite or desirable before they pass to the University; for Milton, however, home-life meant, from the first, not only broad interests and refinement, but active encouragement towards literature and study. In 1625 he left St Paul's. He was not a precocious genius, a 'boy poet,' like Chatterton or Shelley. Of his extant English poems[3] only one, *On the Death of a Fair Infant*, was written in his school-days. But his early training had done that which was all-important: it had laid the foundation of the far-ranging knowledge which makes *Paradise Lost* unique for diversity of suggestion and interest.

Early training.

Milton entered at Christ's College, Cambridge, commencing residence in the Easter term of 1625. Seven years were spent at the University. He took his B.A. degree in 1629, proceeded M.A. in 1632, and in the latter year

At Cambridge.

---

[1] See the article on him in Grove's *Dictionary of Music*.

[2] Milton was very fond of the organ; see *Il Penseroso*, 161, note. During his residence at Horton Milton made occasional journeys to London to hear, and obtain instruction in, music.

[3] His paraphrases of *Psalms* cxiv, cxxxvi, scarcely come under this heading.

left Cambridge. His experience of University life had not been wholly fortunate. He was, and felt himself to be, out of sympathy with his surroundings; and whenever in after-years he spoke of Cambridge[1] it was with something of the grave *impietas* of Gibbon who, unsoftened even by memories of Magdalen, complained that the fourteen months spent at Oxford were the least profitable part of his life. Milton, in fact, anticipates the laments that we find in the correspondence of Gray, addressed sometimes to Richard West and reverberated from the banks of the Isis. It may, however, be fairly assumed that, whether consciously or not, Milton owed a good deal to his University; and it must not be forgotten that the uncomplimentary and oft-quoted allusions to Cambridge date for the most part from the unhappy period when Milton the politician and polemical dogmatist had effectually divorced himself at once from Milton the scholar and Milton the poet. A poet he had proved himself before leaving the University. The short but exquisite ode *At a Solemn Music*, and the *Nativity Hymn* (1629), were already written.

[1] That Milton's feeling towards the authorities of his own college was not entirely unfriendly would appear from the following sentences written in 1642. He takes, he says, the opportunity to "acknowledge publicly, with all grateful mind, that more than ordinary respect which I found, above many of my equals, at the hands of those courteous and learned men, the Fellows of that college wherein I spent some years; who, at my parting after I had taken two degrees, as the manner is, signified many ways how much better it would content them that I would stay; as by many letters full of kindness and loving respect, both before that time and long after, I was assured of their singular good affection towards me."—*Apology for Smectymnuus*, *P. W.* III. 111. Perhaps Cambridge would have been more congenial to Milton had he been sent to Emmanuel College, long a stronghold of Puritanism. Dr John Preston, then Master of the college, was a noted leader of the Puritan party. (Throughout this *Introduction* Milton's prose-works, in Bohn's edition, are referred to under the abbreviation *P. W.*)

Milton's father had settled[1] at Horton in Buckinghamshire.
The five years Thither the son retired in July, 1632. He had
(1632—1637)
spent at Hor- gone to Cambridge with the intention of qualifying
ton. for some profession, perhaps the Church[2]. This
purpose was soon given up, and when Milton returned to his
father's house he seems to have made up his mind that there
was no profession which he cared to enter. He would choose
the better part of studying and preparing himself, by rigorous
self-discipline and application, for the far-off divine event to
which his whole life moved.

It was Milton's constant resolve to achieve something that
The key to should vindicate the ways of God to men, some-
Milton's life. thing great[3] that should justify his own possession
of unique powers—powers of which, with no trace of egotism,
he proclaims himself proudly conscious. The feeling finds
repeated expression in his prose; it is the guiding-star that
shines clear and steadfast even through the mists of politics.
He has a mission to fulfil, a purpose to accomplish, no less

[1] As tenant of the Earl of Bridgewater, according to one account;
but probably the tradition arose from Milton's subsequent connection
with the Bridgewater family.

[2] Cf. Milton's own words, "The Church, to whose service by the
intention of my parents and friends I was destined of a child, and
in my own resolutions." What kept him from taking orders was
not, at first, any difference of belief, but solely his objection to Church
discipline and government. "Coming to some maturity of years, and
perceiving what tyranny had invaded the church, that he who would
take orders must subscribe slave......(I) thought it better to prefer a
blameless silence before the sacred office of speaking, bought and begun
with servitude and forswearing."—*Reason of Church Government*,
P. W. II. 482. Milton disliked in particular the episcopal system,
and spoke of himself as "Church-outed by the prelates."

[3] Cf. the second sonnet; "How soon hath Time." Ten years later
(1641) Milton speaks of the "inward prompting which grew daily upon
me, that by labour and intent study, which I take to be my portion in
this life, joined with the strong propensity of nature, I might perhaps
leave something so written to after times, as they should not willingly
let it die."—*Reason of Church Government, P. W.* II. 477, 478.

than the most fanatic of religious enthusiasts; and the means whereby this end is to be attained are fourfold: devotion to learning, devotion to religion, ascetic purity of life, and the pursuit of σπουδαιότης or "excellent seriousness" of thought.

This period of self-centred isolation lasted from 1632 to 1638. Gibbon tells us among the many wise things contained in that most wise book the *Autobiography*, that every man has two educations: that which he receives from his teachers and that which he owes to himself; the latter being infinitely the more important. During these five years Milton completed his second education; ranging the whole world of classical[1] antiquity and absorbing the classical genius so thoroughly that the ancients were to him what they afterwards became to Landor, what they have never become to any other English poet in the same degree, even as the very breath of his being; learning, too, all of art, especially music, that contemporary England could furnish; wresting from modern literatures (especially Italian[2]) their last secrets; and combining these vast and diverse influences into a splendid equipment of hard-won, well-ordered culture. The world has known many greater scholars in the technical, limited sense than Milton, but few men, if any, who have mastered more things worth mastering in art, letters and scholarship[3]. It says much for the poet that he was sustained through this period of study, pursued *ohne Hast, ohne Rast*, by the full consciousness that all would be crowned by a masterpiece which should add one more testimony to the belief in that God who ordains the fates of men. It says also a very great deal for the father who suffered his son to follow in this manner the path of learning.

[1] He was closely familiar too with post-classical writers like Philo and the neo-Platonists; nor must we forget the mediæval element in his learning, due often to Rabbinical teaching.

[2] Cf. his Italian poems (pp. 5—10).

[3] Milton's poems with their undercurrent of perpetual allusion are the best proof of the width of his reading; but interesting supplementary evidence is afforded by the commonplace book discovered in 1874, and printed by the *Camden Society*, 1876. It contains extracts from about 80 different authors whose works Milton had studied.

True, Milton gave more than one earnest of his future
Milton's lyric fame. The dates of the early pieces—*L'Allegro, Il*
verse; its rela-
tion to contem- *Penseroso, Arcades, Comus* and *Lycidas*—are not
porary life. all certain; but probably each was composed
at Horton before 1638. We have spoken of them elsewhere.
Here we may note that four of them have great autobiographic
value as an indirect commentary, written from Milton's coign
of seclusion, upon the moral crisis through which English life
and thought were passing, the clash between the careless
hedonism of the Cavalier world and the deepening austerity
of Puritanism. In *L'Allegro* the poet holds the balance
almost equal between the two opposing tendencies. In *Il
Penseroso* it becomes clear to which side his sympathies are
leaning. *Comus* is a covert prophecy of the downfall of the
Court-party, while *Lycidas* openly "foretells the ruine" of the
Established Church. The latter poem is the final utterance of
Milton's lyric genius. Here he reaches, in Mr Mark Pattison's
words, the high-water mark of English verse; and then—the
pity of it—he resigns that place among the *lyrici vates* of which
the Roman singer was ambitious, and for nearly twenty years
suffers his lyre to hang mute and rusty in the temple of the
Muses.

The composition of *Lycidas* may be assigned to the year
Travels in 1637. In the spring of the next year Milton started
Italy; close of
the first period for Italy. He had long made himself a master of
in his life. Italian, and it was natural that he should seek
inspiration in the land where many English poets, from
Chaucer to Shelley, have found it. Milton remained abroad
some fifteen months. Originally he had intended to include
Sicily and Greece in his travels, but news of the troubles in
England hastened his return. He was brought face to face
Cause of his with the question whether or not he should bear
return to Eng- his part in the coming struggle; whether without
land.
self-reproach he could lead any longer this life of
learning and indifference to the public weal. He decided as we
might have expected that he would decide, though some good
critics see cause to regret the decision. Milton puts his

position very clearly. "I considered it," he says, "dishonourable to be enjoying myself at my ease in foreign lands, while my countrymen were striking a blow for freedom." And again: "Perceiving that the true way to liberty followed on from these beginnings, inasmuch also as I had so prepared myself from my youth that, above all things, I could not be ignorant what is of Divine and what of human right, I resolved, though I was then meditating certain other matters, to transfer into this struggle all my genius and all the strength of my industry."

The summer of 1639 (July) found Milton back in England. Immediately after his return he wrote the *Epitaphium Damonis*, the beautiful elegy in which he lamented the death of his school friend, Diodati. *Lycidas* was the last of the English lyrics: the *Epitaphium*, which should be studied in close connection with *Lycidas*, the last of the long Latin poems. Thenceforth, for a long spell, the rest was silence, so far as concerned poetry. The period which for all men represents the strength and maturity of manhood, which in the cases of other poets produces the best and most characteristic work, is with Milton a blank. In twenty years he composed no more than a bare handful of Sonnets, and even some of these are infected by the taint of political *animus*. Other interests[1] filled his thoughts—the question of Church-reform, education, marriage, and, above all, politics. *The second period, 1640—1660. Milton abandons poetry.*

Milton's first treatise upon the government of the Established Church (*Of Reformation touching Church-Discipline in England*) appeared in 1641. Others followed in quick succession. The abolition of Episcopacy was the watch-word of the enemies of the Anglican Church—the *delenda est Carthago* cry of Puritanism, and no one enforced the point with greater eloquence than Milton. During 1641 and 1642 he wrote five pamphlets on the subject. Meanwhile he was studying the principles of education. On his return from Italy he had undertaken the training of his nephews. *Pamphlets on the Church and Education.*

[1] Milton seems to have cherished some hope of beginning a great poem as late as 1641—2; probably the latter year marked his final surrender of the scheme.

xvi   INTRODUCTION.

This led to consideration of the best educational methods; and in the *Tractate of Education*, 1644, Milton assumed the part of educational theorist. In the previous year, May, 1643, he married[1]. The marriage proved unfortunate. Its immediate outcome was the pamphlets on Divorce. Clearly he had little leisure for literature proper.

Marriage.

The finest of Milton's prose works, the *Areopagitica*, a plea for the free expression of opinion, was published in 1644. In 1645[2] he edited the first collection of his poems. In 1649 his advocacy of the anti-royalist cause was recognised by the offer of a post under the newly appointed Council of State. His bold vindication of the trial of Charles I., *The Tenure of Kings*, had appeared

Political Pamphlets. Appointment to Latin Secretaryship.

[1] His wife (who was only seventeen) was Mary Powell, eldest daughter of Richard Powell, of Forest Hill, a village some little distance from Oxford. She went to stay with her father in July 1643, and refused to return to Milton; why, it is not certain. She was reconciled to her husband in 1645, bore him four children, and died in 1652, in her twenty-seventh year. No doubt, the scene in *P. L.* x. 909—936, in which Eve begs forgiveness of Adam, reproduced the poet's personal experience, while many passages in *Samson Agonistes* must have been inspired by the same cause.

[2] i.e. old style. The volume was entered on the registers of the Stationers' Company under the date of October 6th, 1645. It was published on Jan. 2, 1645—6, with the following title page:

"*Poems of Mr. John Milton, both English and Latin, compos'd at several times. Printed by his true Copies. The Songs were set in Musick by Mr. Henry Lawes, gentleman of the King's Chappel, and one of His Majesties private Musick.*
'————*Baccare frontem
Cingite, ne vati noceat mala lingua futuro.*' VIRG. *Ecl.* 7.
Printed and publish'd according to Order. London, Printed by Ruth Raworth, for Humphrey Moseley, and are to be sold at the signe of the Princes Arms in Pauls Churchyard. 1645."

From the prefatory Address to the Reader it is clear that the collection was due to the initiative of the publisher. Milton's own feeling is expressed by the motto, where the words "*vati futuro*" show that, as earlier in the same year. Milton accepted the offer, becoming Latin[1] Secretary to the Committee of Foreign Affairs. There was nothing distasteful about his duties. He drew up the despatches to foreign governments, translated state-papers, and served as interpreter to foreign envoys. Had his duties stopped here his acceptance of the post would, I think, have proved an unqualified gain. It brought him into contact with the first men in the state[2], gave him a practical insight *The advantage* into the working of national affairs and the motives *of the post.* of human action; in a word, furnished him with that experience of life which is essential to all poets who aspire to be something more than "the idle singers of an empty day." But unfortunately the secretaryship entailed the necessity of *Its disadvan-* defending at every turn the past course of the *tage.* revolution and the present policy of the Council. Milton, in fact, held a perpetual brief as advocate for his party. Hence the endless and unedifying controversies into which he drifted; controversies which wasted the most precious years of his life, warped, as some critics think, his nature, and eventually cost him his eyesight.

Between 1649 and 1660 Milton produced no less than eleven pamphlets. Several of these arose out of the pub- *Milton's writ-* lication of the famous *Eikon Basilike*. The book *ings on behalf of the Com-* was printed in 1649 and created so extraordinary a *monwealth.*

he judged, his great achievement was yet to come. The volume was divided into two parts, the first containing the English, the second the Latin poems. *Comus* was printed at the close of the former, with a separate title-page to mark its importance.

[1] A Latin Secretary was required because the Council scorned, as Edward Phillips says, "to carry on their affairs in the wheedling, lisping jargon of the cringing French." Milton's salary was £288, in modern money about £900.

[2] There is no proof that Milton ever had personal intercourse with Cromwell, and Mr Mark Pattison implies that he was altogether neglected by the foremost men of the time. Yet it seems unlikely that the Secretary of the Committee should not have been on friendly terms with some of its members, Vane, for example, and Whitelocke.

M. S. *b*

INTRODUCTION.

sensation that Milton was asked to reply to it. This he did with *Eikonoklastes*, introducing the wholly unworthy sneer at Sidney's *Arcadia* and the awkwardly expressed reference to Shakespeare[1]. Controversy of this barren type has the inherent disadvantage that once started it may never end. The Royalists commissioned the Leyden professor, Salmasius, to prepare a counterblast, the *Defensio Regia*, and this in turn was met by Milton's *Pro Populo Anglicano Defensio*, 1651, over the preparation of which he lost what little power of eyesight remained[2]. Salmasius retorted, and died before his second *farrago* of scurrilities was issued: Milton was bound to answer, and the *Defensio Secunda* appeared in 1654. Neither of the combatants gained anything by the dispute; while the subsequent development of the

His blindness.

---

[1] See *L'Allegro*, 133—134, note. It would have been more to the point to remind his readers that the imprisoned king must have spent a good many hours over La Calprenède's *Cassandre*.

[2] Perhaps this was the saddest part of the episode. Milton tells us in the *Defensio Secunda* that his eyesight was injured by excessive study in boyhood: "from the twelfth year of my age I scarce ever left my lessons and went to bed before midnight. This was the first cause of my blindness." Continual reading and writing must have increased the infirmity, and by 1650 the sight of the left eye had gone. He was warned that he must not use the other for book-work. Unfortunately this was just the time when the Commonwealth stood most in need of his services. If Milton had not written the first *Defence* he might have retained his partial vision. The choice lay between private good and public duty. He repeated in 1650 the sacrifice of 1639. "In such a case I could not listen to the physician, not if Æsculapius himself had spoken from his sanctuary; I could not but obey that inward monitor, I know not what, that spoke to me from heaven......I concluded to employ the little remaining eyesight I was to enjoy in doing this, the greatest service to the common weal it was in my power to render" (*Second Defence*). By the Spring of 1652 Milton was quite blind. He was then in his forty-fourth year. Probably the disease from which he suffered was amaurosis. See the *Appendix* (pp. 120, 121) on *P. L.* III. 22—26. Throughout *P. L.* and *Samson Agonistes* there are frequent references to his affliction.

controversy in which Milton crushed the Amsterdam pastor and professor, Morus, goes far to prove the contention of Mr Mark Pattison, that it was an evil day when the poet left his study at Horton to do battle for the Commonwealth amid the vulgar brawls of the market-place:

"Not here, O Apollo,
Were haunts meet for thee."

Fortunately this poetic interregnum in Milton's life was not destined to last much longer. The Restoration came, a blessing in disguise, and in 1660[1] the ruin of Milton's political[2] party and of his personal hopes, the absolute overthrow of the cause for which he had fought for twenty years, left him free. The author of *Lycidas* could once more become a poet. *The Restoration releases Milton from politics. Return to poetry.*

Much has been written upon this second period, 1639—1660, and a word may be said here. We saw what parting of the ways confronted Milton on his return from Italy. Did he choose aright? Should he have continued upon the path of learned leisure? There are writers who argue that Milton made a mistake. A poet, they say, should keep clear of political strife: fierce controversy can benefit no man: who touches pitch must expect to be, certainly will be, defiled: Milton sacrificed twenty of the best years of his life, doing work which an underling could have done and which was not worth doing: another *Comus* might have been written, a loftier *Lycidas:* that literature should be the poorer by the absence of these possible masterpieces, that the second greatest genius which England has produced should in a way be the "inheritor of unfulfilled renown," is and must be a thing entirely and terribly deplorable. This is the view of the purely literary critic. Mr Mark Pattison writes very much to this effect. *Should Milton have kept apart from political life? One reply to this question.*

[1] The date 1660 must not be pressed too closely. As a matter of strict detail, Milton probably began *Paradise Lost* in 1658; but it was not till the Restoration in 1660 that he definitely resigned all his political hopes, and became quite free to realise his poetical ambition.

[2] The changes in his political views cannot be traced here.

INTRODUCTION.

There remains the other side of the question. It may fairly be contended that had Milton elected in 1639 to live the scholar's life apart from "the action of men," *Paradise Lost*, as we have it, could never have been written[1]. Knowledge of life and human nature, insight into the problems of men's motives and emotions, grasp of the broader issues of the human tragedy, all these were essential to the author of an epic poem; they could only be obtained through commerce with the world; they would have remained beyond the reach of a recluse. Dryden complained that Milton saw nature through the spectacles of books: we might have had to complain that he saw men through the same medium. Fortunately it is not so: and it is not so because at the age of thirty-two he threw in his fortunes with those of his country; like the diver in Schiller's ballad he took the plunge which was to cost him so dear. The mere man of letters will never move the world. Æschylus fought at Marathon: Shakespeare was practical to the tips of his fingers; a better business man than Goethe there was not within a radius of a hundred miles of Weimar.

Milton's own opinion. This aspect of the question is emphasised by Milton himself. The man, he says, "who would not be frustrate of his hope to write well hereafter in laudable things, ought himself to be a true poem, that is, a composition and pattern of the best and honourablest things, *not*[2] *presuming to sing high praises of heroic men or famous cities, unless he have within himself the experience and the practice of all that which is praiseworthy.*" Again, in estimating the qualifications which the writer of an epic such as he contemplated should possess, he is careful to include "insight into all seemly and generous arts and *affairs*[3]."

How politics may have influenced the poet. Truth usually lies half-way between extremes: perhaps it does so here. No doubt, Milton did gain very greatly by breathing awhile the larger air of public life, even though that air was often tainted by

---

[1] This is true of *Samson Agonistes* too.   [2] The italics are mine.
[3] *Reason of Church Government, P. W.* II. 481.

much impurity. No doubt, too, twenty years of contention must have left their mark even on Milton. In one of the very few places[1] where he "abides our question," Shakespeare writes:

> O! for my sake do you with Fortune chide,
> The guilty goddess of my harmful deeds,
> That did not better for my life provide,
> Than public means, which public manners breeds:
> Thence comes it that my name receives a brand;
> And almost thence my nature is subdu'd
> To what it works in, like the dyer's hand.

Milton's genius was subdued in this way. If we compare him, the Milton of the great epics and of *Samson Agonistes*, with Homer or Shakespeare—and none but the greatest can be his parallel—we find in him a certain want of humanity, a touch of narrowness. He lacks the large-heartedness, the genial, generous breadth of Shakespeare; the sympathy and sense of the *lacrimæ rerum* that even in *Troilus and Cressida* or *Timon of Athens* are there for those who have eyes wherewith to see them. Milton reflects many of the less gracious aspects of Puritanism, its intolerance, want of humour, one-sided intensity. He is stern and austere, and it seems natural to assume that this narrowness was to a great extent the price he paid for twenty years of ceaseless special pleading and dispute. The real misfortune of his life lay in the fact that he fell on evil, angry days when there was no place for moderate men. He had to be one of two things: either a controversialist or a student: there was no *via media*. Probably he chose aright; but we could wish that the conditions under which he chose had been different.

The last part of Milton's life, 1660—1674, passed quietly. At the age of fifty-two he was thrown back upon poetry, and could at length discharge his self-imposed obligation. The early poems he had never regarded as a fulfilment of the debt due to his Creator.

From the Restoration to Milton's death.

---

[1] *Sonnet* CXI.

Even when the fire of political strife burned at its hottest, Milton did not forget the purpose which he had conceived in his boyhood. Of that purpose *Paradise Lost* was the full attainment. We need not trace its history here. It suffices to observe that the poem was begun about 1658; was finished in 1663, the year of Milton's third[1] marriage; revised from 1663 to 1665; and eventually issued in 1667. Before its publication Milton had commenced (in the autumn of 1665) its sequel *Paradise Regained*, which in turn was closely followed by *Samson Agonistes*. The completion of *Paradise Regained* may be assigned to the year 1666—that of *Samson Agonistes* to 1667. Some time was spent in their revision; and in January, 1671, they were published together, in a single volume.

Close of Milton's life. In 1673 Milton brought out a reprint of the 1645 edition of his *Poems*, adding most of the sonnets written in the interval. The last four years of his life were devoted to prose works of no particular interest to us[2]. He continued to live in London. His third marriage had proved happy, and he enjoyed something of the renown which was rightly his. Various well-known men used to visit him—notably Dryden[3], who on one of his visits asked and received

---

[1] Milton's second marriage took place in the autumn of 1656, i.e. after he had become blind. His wife died in February, 1658. Cf. the *Sonnet*, "Methought I saw my late espoused saint," the pathos of which is heightened by the fact that he had never seen her.

[2] The treatise on *Christian Doctrine* is valuable as throwing much light on the theological views expressed in the two epic poems and *Samson Agonistes*. The discovery of the MS. of this treatise in 1823 gave Macaulay an opportunity of writing his famous essay on Milton.

[3] The lines by Dryden which were printed beneath the portrait of Milton in Tonson's folio edition of *Paradise Lost* published in 1688 are too familiar to need quotation; but it is worth noting that the younger poet had in Milton's lifetime described the great epic as "one of the most noble, and most sublime poems which either this age or nation has produced" (preface to *The State of Innocence*, 1674). Further, tradition assigned to Dryden (a Roman Catholic and a Royalist) the remark, "this fellow (Milton) cuts us all out and the ancients too."

permission to dramatise¹ *Paradise Lost*. It does not often happen that a university can point to two such poets among her living sons, each without rival in his generation.

Milton died in 1674, November 8th. He was buried in St Giles' Church, Cripplegate. When we think of him *His death.* we have to think of a man who lived a life of very singular purity and devotion to duty; who for what he conceived to be his country's good sacrificed—and no one can well estimate the sacrifice—during twenty years the aim that was nearest to his heart and best suited to his genius; who, however, eventually realised his desire of writing a great work *in gloriam Dei.*

[1] See Marvell's "Commendatory Verses," 17—30, to *Paradise Lost.*

MILTON'S SONNETS.

The Sonnets: when published. Ten of the sonnets were published in the first edition of Milton's minor poems (1645). Of the other thirteen, composed between 1645 and 1658, nine appeared in the second edition of the minor poems (1673). Four of them (XV., XVI., XVII.[1], XXII.) it was inexpedient to publish then on account of their political tone. They were printed in 1694 by Edward Phillips in the volume containing his *Life* of Milton and translation of the *Letters of State*. The history of all the sonnets, so far as it is known, is given in the *Notes*.

Types of Sonnet: In respect of structure, there are two main types of sonnet in English—the Petrarchan and the Shakespearean: Milton's sonnets belong, substantially, to the former; he speaks of his second sonnet as written "in a Petrarchian" manner[2].

The Petrarchan. The Petrarchan sonnet is the more elaborate. It is composed of two systems, the octave and the sestet, between which a certain balance of thought and cadence must be maintained. The first eight lines (the octave) are so regulated by the prescribed disposition of the rhymes[3] as to form one long movement, broken only by a slight pause at the end of the fourth line. The marked pause[4] at the close of this

---

[1] Sonnet XVII. had appeared previously in a *Life* of Vane; see p. 51.

[2] See p. 31.

[3] Lines 1, 4, 5, 8 rhyme; and lines 2, 3, 6, 7. The rhyme of the first and eighth lines binds together the whole octave, making one movement of the eight verses.

[4] The one important respect in which Milton diverges from the Petrarchan sonnet is his neglect of this pause. In about half his sonnets he carries on the thought and rhythm of the octave into the sestet without any break. See sonnets I., XI., XII., XVI., XVII., XVIII., XIX., XXII., XXIII. Also he often has no pause at the end of the fourth line; in the Petrarchan sonnet this pause is of much less consequence than the other.

movement necessarily makes a climax: the sonnet reaches its high-water point of thought and rhythm, and then falls gradually away. The sestet continues, but adds no fresh element to the thought embodied in the octave, and its rhythm is of a simpler character, suggesting an impression of leaving off. The sestet, in fact, is subordinate to the octave. Its disposition of rhymes is not limited so strictly: but the last two lines may not form a rhymed couplet.

The Shakespearean sonnet[1] is less complex. It consists merely of four quatrains of alternate rhyme, rounded off with a rhymed distich at the end[2]. *The Shakespearean.* It presents no equivalent to the prolonged and involved movement of the Petrarchan octave, or to the adjustment between the octave and the sestet. Structurally there is no reason why any marked pause should occur regularly at one particular place in the first twelve lines: the three quatrains may be of equal importance. Hence the climax is deferred till the end. It comes in the final couplet, which from its position and its rhyme takes to itself the main emphasis of the poem. And herein, according to many critics, lies the great objection to the Shakespearean sonnet. The interest (they say) of a sonnet should be spread over the whole, not concentrated in a single couplet as though the piece were an epigram.

It is scarcely profitable, however, to disparage the Shakespearean sonnet, with Shakespeare's work before us to shew what exquisite possibilities it offers. *Different qualities of the two types.* Rather, we should recognise that the two types of sonnet possess different qualities[3]—the Shakespearean sonnet

[1] It is so called because Shakespeare's sonnets are the most famous examples of the type; he did not invent it. It was used also by Thomas Watson, Drayton, Drummond, and many Elizabethans. Hallam speaks of "a scanty number of Italian precedents" for this form (*Literature of Europe*, III. 265, ed. 1879).

[2] Only one (XVI.) of Milton's sonnets ends thus.

[3] "The quest of the Shakespearean sonnet is not, like that of the sonnet of octave and sestet, sonority, but sweetness"—*Theodore Watts.*

the quality of sweetness, and the Petrarchan the quality of complex harmony. And we may perhaps add that, differing thus in kind, they ought accordingly to be made to serve different purposes. The Shakespearean sonnet seems more adapted to a series in which the same theme is treated from different aspects. The sonnet then becomes a stanza almost, and in a series of stanzas read consecutively something simpler than the carefully balanced octave and sestet is required. This is supplied by the arrangement of the three quatrains finished off with that rhymed couplet which the ear gets to anticipate and were loth to miss. On the other hand, where a sonnet stands independent, the individual and complete expression of some single thought or fancy, there is scope for a more involved mechanism. All[1] Milton's sonnets, it will be observed, are of this individual character. Each handles one main idea in such a way as to be self-sufficing; there is no dependence on anything that precedes or follows. Herein he is unlike the Elizabethan sonnetteers, many of whom composed sonnet-sequences[2]. He is unlike them too in his choice of themes and in his straightforward lucidity of style. On these points Mr Mark Pattison has the following admirable summary:—

The subjects and style of Milton's sonnets.

"The effectiveness of Milton's sonnets is chiefly due to the *real* nature of the character, person, or incident of which each is the delineation. Each person, thing, or fact, is a moment in Milton's life, on which he was stirred; sometimes in the soul's depths, sometimes on the surface of feeling, but always truly moved. He found the sonnet enslaved to a single theme, that of unsuccessful love, mostly a simulated passion. He emancipated it, and, as Landor says, gave the 'notes to glory.'

---

[1] Sonnet XII. is only an apparent exception. It may be read independently of XI., though it gains by being taken in connection therewith.

[2] Cf. Spenser's *Amoretti;* Sidney's *Astrophel and Stella;* Constable's *Diana;* Watson's *Tears of Fancie;* Drayton's *Idea;* and several minor collections which Professor Arber has republished in his *English Garner*, vols. V.—VII.

And what is here felt powerfully, is expressed directly and simply. The affectation of the Elizabethan sonnet, its elaborate artifice, is discarded, and replaced by a manly straightforwardness...The sonnet, the most artificial of our poetic forms, here, for the first time in English, offers its purport with the simplicity of blank verse. Previous English sonnetteers seem to have thought it necessary to match the complexity of the form with an equally elaborate involution of the sense. Their sonnets are works of ingenuity, offering a problem to the intelligence, rather than an excitant to the imagination...After his first essay, Sonnet I., Milton threw aside the fashionable model of the preceding age. In all his sonnets there is not a proposition of which the meaning is doubtful, or the construction intricate. He chose deliberately to write thus, when the weight of the precedent of the English sonnet was the other way, and when it was considered to be essential to that form of poem to eschew the direct and the obvious. It is the glory of the Miltonic sonnet that being based upon what is common and simple it attains to the high and noble[1]."

Milton's Sonnets may be divided into three groups, "the controversial," "the personal," and "the political." *Three Groups of the Sonnets.* The first of these groups (Sonnets XI., XII. and "The New Forcers") are the least interesting, at once from the nature of their several subjects and the grim ungainliness that usually characterises Milton's attempts *Controversial.* at humour. To the other groups Mr Stopford Brooke introduces us thus:

"The *personal sonnets* have great and solemn beauty, the beauty that belongs to the revelation of a great spirit. We may well compare the second sonnet, *Personal.* with its quiet self-confidence, its resolved humility, its aspiration to perform the great Task-master's work, with the sonnet written, twenty years after, on his blindness, in 1652. It looks back

---

[1] This criticism is not, of course, meant to apply to the three controversial Sonnets, which, as has been happily said, "are less poetry than rhymed passages from the polemical treatises." But the criticism is eminently true of the Miltonic Sonnet in general.

over many sorrows and tumults to the earlier one; and, depressed by his blindness, he thinks how little has been, and may now be done; but deep religious patience helps him to think that God works, and that 'They also serve who only stand and wait.' Not less noble in thought, not less stately in expression, but full of the veteran's consciousness of work, is the sonnet written three years later to Cyriack Skinner, also on his blindness. He does not bate one jot of hope, but steers right onward... The sonnet written when the Assault was intended to the City, and three others, written to Lawes, and Mr Lawrence, and Cyriack Skinner, may also be called personal[1]. They show Milton in his artist nature as the poet who knew his own worth; as the lover of music and as the musician; the lover of Italy, of Dante's poem, and of Tuscan airs; the tender friend; the lover of classic verse. No sonnets in the English tongue come nearer than those to Lawrence and Cyriack Skinner to the mingled festivity and serious grace of Horace, and their religious spirit, graver than that of Horace, makes them Miltonic.

"Of the *political sonnets*, the finest[2] is that to Cromwell.

Political. Those to Fairfax and Vane are 'noble odes,' but that to Cromwell is written like an organ song by Handel in his triumphant hour. More solemn still, and justly called a psalm, is the stern and magnificent summons to God to avenge His slaughtered saints, slain by the bloody Piedmontese. It is harsh, some have said; nay, it is of great Nature herself: it has 'a voice whose sound is like the sea.'"

---

[1] I think that we may put Sonnets IX., X., XIV., XXIII. under this heading, though Mr Brooke (whose classification I have followed, except in this point) groups them together in a separate class depicting "four beautiful types of womanhood."

[2] More often, I fancy, the palm is awarded to Sonnet XVIII.

A SELECTION OF CRITICISMS ON MILTON'S SONNETS[1].

JOHNSON: "The *Sonnets* were written in different parts of Milton's life, upon different occasions. They deserve not any particular criticism; for of the best it can only be said, that they are not bad; and perhaps only the eighth[2] and the twenty-first[3] are truly entitled to this slender commendation. The fabrick of a sonnet, however adapted to the Italian language, has never succeeded in ours, which, having greater variety of termination, requires the rhymes to be often changed.

Those little pieces may be dispatched without much anxiety; a greater work calls for greater care[4]. I am now to examine *Paradise Lost*; a poem, which, considered with respect to design, may claim the first place, and with respect to performance the second, among the productions of the human mind" (*Life* of Milton).

Boswell records "a lively saying of Dr Johnson to Miss Hannah More, who had expressed a wonder that the poet who had written *Paradise Lost*, should write such poor sonnets: 'Milton, madam, was a genius that could cut a Colossus from a rock, but could not carve heads upon cherry-stones'" (*Life* of Johnson, under the year 1784, Napier's ed. IV. 392).

---

[1] I have thought that it would add much to the value of this volume if what is said or quoted in the foregoing pages were supplemented in the present edition (1904) by a tolerably representative *résumé* of critical opinion on the Sonnets.

[2] "When the Assault."

[3] "To Cyriack Skinner."

[4] In fairness to Johnson one must quote the remainder of the paragraph, which proves that he was not insensible to Milton's greatness. It is mainly in his treatment of Milton's minor poems that Johnson is so depreciatory and infelicitous. See *Introductions* to *Comus*, pp. xl, xli, xliv, xlv, and *Lycidas*, pp. xlvi, xlvii (Pitt Press eds.).

MACAULAY[1]: "Traces of the peculiar character of Milton may be found in all his works; but it is most strongly displayed in the Sonnets. Those remarkable poems have been undervalued by critics who have not understood their nature. They have no epigrammatic point. There is none of the ingenuity of Filicaja[2] in the thought, none of the hard and brilliant enamel of Petrarch in the style. They are simple but majestic records of the feelings of the poet; as little tricked out for the public eye as his diary would have been[3]. A victory, an unexpected attack upon the city, a momentary fit of depression or exultation, a jest thrown out against one of his books, a dream which for a short time restored to him that beautiful face over which the grave had closed for ever, led him to musings which, without effort, shaped themselves into verse. The unity of sentiment and severity of style which characterise these little pieces remind us of the Greek Anthology, or perhaps still more of the Collects of the Anglican Liturgy. The noble poem on the Massacres of Piedmont is strictly a Collect in verse.

The Sonnets are more or less striking, according as the occasions which gave birth to them are more or less interesting. But they are, almost without exception, dignified by a sobriety and greatness of mind to which we know not where to look for a parallel. It would, indeed, be scarcely safe to draw any decided inferences as to the character of a writer from passages

[1] The fashion is to sneer at Macaulay as a critic. One has all the more pleasure therefore in citing a passage which, written in 1825, shows that to Macaulay belongs the credit of being one of the first (if not *the* first) of prose-critics to do justice to Milton's Sonnets and reverse the 18th century verdict, as expressed by Johnson and Steevens.

[2] The Italian lyrical poet (1642—1707). "Some of his patriotic sonnets are famous; but his verse, though not without beauty and spirit, is disfigured by the rhetorical tricks and false conceits of the period."—*Chambers's Encyclopædia*. One of Filicaia's Sonnets is rendered in *Childe Harold* IV. xlii ("Italia! oh, Italia"), xliii.

[3] From the Cambridge MSS, with their numerous corrections, we see that the seeming simplicity of the Sonnets is really the art that conceals art.

directly egotistical. But the qualities which we have ascribed to Milton[1], though perhaps most strongly marked in those parts of his works which treat of his personal feelings, are distinguishable in every page, and impart to all his writings, prose and poetry, English, Latin, and Italian, a strong family likeness."

HALLAM: "The Sonnets of Milton have obtained of late years the admiration of all real lovers of poetry. Johnson has been as impotent to fix the public taste in this instance as in his other criticisms on the smaller poems of the author or *Paradise Lost*. These Sonnets are indeed unequal; the expression is sometimes harsh, and sometimes obscure; sometimes too much of pedantic allusion interferes with the sentiment, nor am I reconciled to his frequent deviations from the best Italian structure. But such blemishes are lost in the majestic simplicity, the holy calm, that ennoble many of these short compositions."

MASSON: "An early student of the Italian poets, Milton had learnt the true music of the Sonnet from Petrarch most of all, so that, when he first ventured on trials of the Sonnet-form in English, he thought of it as the 'Petrarchian Stanza.' These first trials were made while he was still a Cambridge student, long before that 'damp' fell round his path of which Wordsworth speaks as being already round it when he seized the Sonnet and the thing in his hands became a trumpet. The series of his Sonnets, however, though beginning about 1630, extends to 1658; and most of them *were* those 'soul-animating strains' which he blew at intervals from this instrument when other poetry was in forced abeyance from him, and he was engrossed in prose polemics. Milton's last sixteen Sonnets, indeed, with a verse or two besides, are the few occasional strains that connect, as by intermittent trumpet-blasts through twenty years, the rich minor poetry of his youth and early manhood with the greater poetry of his declining age in blindness after the Restoration."

COURTHOPE: "Milton...returned home [from Italy] to find the tide of anti-Episcopal feeling in England running at its height,

---

[1] e.g. "The character of Milton was peculiarly distinguished by loftiness of spirit... His temper was serious, perhaps stern."

and, with the powerful Puritan bias in his nature, he felt that he must take part in the conflict. It is evident, from what he says in [his *Reason of Church Government*, 1641], that he did not expect to be long detained from the pursuit of the art to which he was devoted, and had no suspicion that for nearly twenty years he would be plunged into a whirlpool of controversy and civil conflict, in which the only outlet for his imagination would be found in the composition of his sonnets. These, from the biographical point of view alone, are of the highest value. They fall readily into distinct classes; some being purely personal in feeling, such as vii, xix, xxii, xxiii; others being written in compliment to friends, such as those to *A Virtuous Young Lady; The Lady Margaret Ley; H. Lawes; Cyriac Skinner; Mr Lawrence;* or *The Memory of Mrs Catherine Thomson;* the largest group having its origin in the praise of party leaders, or in passing phases of religious and political warfare, the most notable of which are viii, xi, xii, xv, xvi, xvii, xviii, and the irregular sonnet *On the New Forcers of Conscience under the Long Parliament*. Read in the light of the dates of their composition, and in connection with the numerous prose pamphlets written by Milton from 1641 to 1658, the sonnets furnish the key to the development of his genius between the day when he bade farewell to pastoral poetry and that on which he began to lay the foundation of *Paradise Lost*."

"The Spectator" (August 18, 1883): "The sweetness of the early sonnetteers is not to be found in Milton. For the first time in our sonnet literature all artifice has disappeared. He has used the form to express personal feeling, and even ardent passion, but not the passion of love. Ingenuity of fancy is discarded, there are no conceits in these poems, and no sign that Milton used the sonnet as a conventional form of verse.... Milton, who ranks with the greatest writers of sonnets, is uniformly intelligible. He knows what he wishes to utter, and expresses it with what may seem bald simplicity, but is in truth the perfection of art.... A sonnet with one obscure line lacks the perfection we are entitled to look for in so short a poem."

MILTON'S SONNETS.

I.

TO THE NIGHTINGALE.

O NIGHTINGALE, that on yon bloomy spray
    Warblest at eve, when all the woods are still;
    Thou with fresh hope the lover's heart dost fill,
    While the jolly hours lead on propitious May:
Thy liquid notes that close the eye of day,   5
    First heard before the shallow cuckoo's bill,
    Portend success in love; Oh, if Jove's will
    Have linked that amorous power to thy soft lay,
Now timely sing, ere the rude bird of hate
    Foretell my hopeless doom in some grove nigh;   10
    As thou from year to year hast sung too late
For my relief, yet hadst no reason why:
    Whether the Muse, or Love, call thee his mate,
    Both them I serve, and of their train am I.

II.

ON HIS BEING ARRIVED TO THE AGE OF TWENTY-THREE.

How soon hath Time, the subtle thief of youth,
    Stolen on his wing my three-and-twentieth year!
    My hasting days fly on with full career,
    But my late spring no bud or blossom shew'th.
Perhaps my semblance might deceive the truth,
    That I to manhood am arrived so near;
    And inward ripeness doth much less appear,
    That some more timely-happy spirits endu'th.
Yet be it less or more, or soon or slow,
    It shall be still in strictest measure even
    To that same lot, however mean or high,
Toward which Time leads me, and the will of Heaven;
    All is, if I have grace to use it so,
    As ever in my great Task-Master's eye.

III.

Donna leggiadra, il cui bel nome onora
    L' erbosa val di Reno e il nobil varco,
    Bene è colui d' ogni valore scarco
    Qual tuo spirto gentil non innamora,
Che dolcemente mostra si di fuora,   5
    De' sui atti soavi giammai parco,
    E i don', che son d' amor saette ed arco,
    Laonde l' alta tua virtù s' infiora.
Quando tu vaga parli, o lieta canti,
    Che mover possa duro alpestre legno,   10
    Guardi ciascun a gli occhi ed a gli orecchi
L' entrata chi di te si truova indegno;
    Grazia sola di sù gli vaglia, innanti
    Che 'l disio amoroso al cuor s' invecchi.

IV.

Qual in colle aspro, al imbrunir di sera,
    L' avvezza giovinetta pastorella
    Va bagnando l' erbetta strana e bella
    Che mal si spande a disusata spera,
Fuor di sua natia alma primavera,
    Così Amor meco insù la lingua snella
    Desta il fior novo di strania favella,
    Mentre io di te, vezzosamente altera,
Canto, dal mio buon popol non inteso,
    E 'l bel Tamigi cangio col bel Arno.
    Amor lo volse, ed io, a l' altrui peso,
Seppi ch' Amor cosa mai volse indarno.
    Deh! foss' il mio cuor lento e' l duro seno
    A chi pianta dal ciel si buon terreno.

CANZONE.

Ridonsi donne e giovani amorosi,
M' accostandosi attorno, e 'Perchè scrivi,
Perchè tu scrivi in lingua ignota e strana,
Verseggiando d' amor, e come t' osi?
Dinne, se la tua speme sia mai vana,   5
E de' pensieri lo miglior t' arrivi!'
Così mi van burlando: 'altri rivi,
Altri lidi t' aspettan, ed altre onde,
Nelle cui verdi sponde
Spuntati ad or ad or a la tua chioma   10
L' immortal guiderdon d' eterne frondi.
Perchè alle spalle tue soverchia soma?'
    Canzon, dirotti, e tu per me rispondi:
'Dice mia Donna, e 'l suo dir è il mio cuore,
"Questa è lingua di cui si vanta Amore."'   15

V.

Diodati (e te 'l dirò con maraviglia),
    Quel ritroso io, ch' amor spreggiar solea
    E de' suoi lacci spesso mi ridea,
    Già caddi, ov' uom dabben talor s' impiglia.
Nè treccie d' oro, nè guancia vermiglia
    M' abbaglian sì, ma sotto nova idea
    Pellegrina bellezza che 'l cuor bea,
    Portamenti alti onesti, e nelle ciglia
Quel sereno fulgor d' amabil nero,
    Parole adorne di lingua più d' una,
    E 'l cantar che di mezzo l' emispero
Traviar ben può la faticosa Luna;
    E degli occhi suoi avventa sì gran fuoco
    Che l' incerar gli orecchi mi fia poco.

VI.

Per certo i bei vostr' occhi, Donna mia,
    Esser non può che non sian lo mio sole;
    Sì mi percuoton forte, come ei suole
    Per l' arene di Libia chi s' invia,
Mentre un caldo vapor (nè sentì pria)   5
    Da quel lato si spinge ove mi duole,
    Che forse amanti nelle lor parole
    Chiaman sospir; io non so che si sia.
Parte rinchiusa e turbida si cela
    Scossomi il petto, e poi n' uscendo poco   10
    Quivi d' attorno o s' agghiaccia o s' ingiela;
Ma quanto agli occhi giunge a trovar loco
    Tutte le notti a me suol far piovose,
    Finchè mia alba rivien colma di rose.

VII.

Giovane, piano, e semplicetto amante,
    Poichè fuggir me stesso in dubbio sono,
    Madonna, a voi del mio cuor l' umil dono
    Farò divoto. Io certo a prove tante
L' ebbi fedele, intrepido, costante,
    Di pensieri leggiadro, accorto, e buono.
    Quando rugge il gran mondo, e scocca il tuono,
    S' arma di se, e d' intero diamante,
Tanto del forse e d' invidia sicuro,
    Di timori, e speranze al popol use,
    Quanto d' ingegno e d' alto valor vago,
E di cetra sonora, e delle Muse.
    Sol troverete in tal parte men duro
    Ove Amor mise l' insanabil ago.

VIII.

WHEN THE ASSAULT WAS INTENDED TO THE CITY.

CAPTAIN, or Colonel, or Knight in arms,
    Whose chance on these defenceless doors may seize,
    If deed of honour did thee ever please,
    Guard them, and him within protect from harms.
He can requite thee; for he knows the charms   5
    That call fame on such gentle acts as these,
    And he can spread thy name o'er lands and seas,
    Whatever clime the sun's bright circle warms.
Lift not thy spear against the Muses' bower:
    The great Emathian conqueror bid spare   10
    The house of Pindarus, when temple and tower
Went to the ground; and the repeated air
    Of sad Electra's poet had the power
    To save the Athenian walls from ruin bare.

IX.

TO A VIRTUOUS YOUNG LADY.

Lady, that in the prime of earliest youth
    Wisely hast shunned the broad way and the green,
    And with those few art eminently seen
    That labour up the hill of heavenly Truth;
The better part with Mary and with Ruth
    Chosen thou hast; and they that overween,
    And at thy growing virtues fret their spleen,
    No anger find in thee, but pity and ruth.
Thy care is fixed, and zealously attends
    To fill thy odorous lamp with deeds of light,
    And hope that reaps not shame. Therefore be sure
Thou, when the Bridegroom with his feastful friends
    Passes to bliss at the mid-hour of night,
    Hast gained thy entrance, Virgin wise and pure.

X.

TO THE LADY MARGARET LEY.

DAUGHTER to that good Earl, once President
    Of England's Council and her Treasury,
    Who lived in both unstained with gold or fee,
    And left them both, more in himself content,
Till the sad breaking of that Parliament
    Broke him, as that dishonest victory
    At Chæronea, fatal to liberty,
    Killed with report that old man eloquent;
Though later born than to have known the days
    Wherein your father flourished, yet by you,
    Madam, methinks I see him living yet:
So well your words his noble virtues praise
    That all both judge you to relate them true
    And to possess them, honoured Margaret.

XI.

ON THE DETRACTION WHICH FOLLOWED UPON MY WRITING CERTAIN TREATISES.

A BOOK was writ of late called *Tetrachordon*,
    And woven close, both matter, form, and style;
    The subject new: it walked the town a while,
    Numbering good intellects; now seldom pored on.
Cries the stall-reader, "Bless us! what a word on   5
    A title-page is this!"; and some in file
    Stand spelling false, while one might walk to Mile-
    End Green. Why, is it harder, sirs, than *Gordon*,
Colkitto, or *Macdonnel*, or *Galasp?*
    Those rugged names to our like mouths grow sleek 10
    That would have made Quintilian stare and gasp.
Thy age, like ours, O soul of Sir John Cheek,
    Hated not learning worse than toad or asp,
    When thou taught'st Cambridge and King Edward Greek.

XII.

ON THE SAME.

I D but prompt the age to quit their clogs
By the known rules of ancient liberty,
When straight a barbarous noise environs me
Of owls and cuckoos, asses, apes, and dogs;
When those hinds that were transformed to frogs   5
Railed at Latona's twin-born progeny,
Which after held the sun and moon in fee.
But this is got by casting pearl to hogs,
 bawl for freedom in their senseless mood,
And still revolt when Truth would set them free.   10
Licence they mean when they cry Liberty;
Who loves that must first be wise and good:
But from that mark how far they rove we see,
For all this waste of wealth and loss of blood.

XIII.

TO MR H. LAWES ON HIS AIRS.

HARRY, whose tuneful and well-measured song
    First taught our English music how to span
    Words with just note and accent, not to scan
    With Midas' ears, committing short and long,
Thy worth and skill exempts thee from the throng,
    With praise enough for Envy to look wan;
    To after age thou shalt be writ the man
    That with smooth air couldst humour best our tongue.
Thou honour'st verse, and verse must lend her wing
    To honour thee, the priest of Phœbus' quire,
    That tunest their happiest lines in hymn or story.
Dante shall give Fame leave to set thee higher
    Than his Casella, whom he wooed to sing,
    Met in the milder shades of Purgatory.

XIV.

ON THE RELIGIOUS MEMORY OF MRS CATHERINE THOMSON, MY CHRISTIAN FRIEND, DECEASED DEC. 16, 1646.

When Faith and Love, which parted from thee never,
    Had ripened thy just soul to dwell with God,
    Meekly thou didst resign this earthy load
Of death, called life, which us from life doth sever.
Thy works, and alms, and all thy good endeavour,   5
    Stayed not behind, nor in the grave were trod;
    But, as Faith pointed with her golden rod,
Followed thee up to joy and bliss for ever.
Love led them on; and Faith, who knew them best
    Thy handmaids, clad them o'er with purple beams   10
    And azure wings, that up they flew so drest,
And spake the truth of thee on glorious themes
    Before the Judge; who thenceforth bid thee rest,
    And drink thy fill of pure immortal streams.

XV.

TO THE LORD GENERAL FAIRFAX, AT THE SIEGE OF COLCHESTER.

FAIRFAX, whose name in arms through Europe rings,
    Filling each mouth with envy or with praise,
    And all her jealous monarchs with amaze,
    And rumours loud that daunt remotest kings;
Thy firm unshaken virtue ever brings
    Victory home, though new rebellions raise
    Their Hydra heads, and the false North displays
    Her broken league to imp their serpent wings.
O yet a nobler task awaits thy hand
    (For what can war but endless war still breed?)
    Till truth and right from violence be freed,
And public faith cleared from the shameful brand
    Of public fraud. In vain doth Valour bleed,
    While Avarice and Rapine share the land.

XVI.

TO THE LORD GENERAL CROMWELL,

ON THE PROPOSALS OF CERTAIN MINISTERS AT THE COMMITTEE FOR PROPAGATION OF THE GOSPEL.

CROMWELL, our chief of men, who through a cloud
    Not of war only, but detractions rude,
    Guided by faith and matchless fortitude,
    To peace and truth thy glorious way hast ploughed,
And on the neck of crowned Fortune proud   5
    Hast reared God's trophies, and his work pursued,
    While Darwen stream, with blood of Scots imbrued,
    And Dunbar field, resounds thy praises loud,
And Worcester's laureate wreath: yet much remains
    To conquer still; Peace hath her victories   10
    No less renowned than War: new foes arise,
Threatening to bind our souls with secular chains.
    Help us to save free conscience from the paw
    Of hireling wolves, whose Gospel is their maw.

XVII.

TO SIR HENRY VANE THE YOUNGER.

VANE, young in years, but in sage counsel old,
    Than whom a better senator ne'er held
    The helm of Rome, when gowns, not arms, repelled
    The fierce Epirot and the African bold;
Whether to settle peace, or to unfold   5
    The drift of hollow states hard to be spelled;
    Then to advise how war may best upheld
    Move by her two main nerves, iron and gold,
In all her equipage; besides, to know
    Both spiritual power and civil, what each means,   10
    What severs each, thou hast learned, which few have done.
The bounds of either sword to thee we owe:
    Therefore on thy firm hand Religion leans
    In peace, and reckons thee her eldest son.

XVIII.

ON THE LATE MASSACRE IN PIEMONT.

Avenge, O Lord, thy slaughtered saints, whose bones
    Lie scattered on the Alpine mountains cold;
    Even them who kept thy truth so pure of old,
    When all our fathers worshipped stocks and stones,
Forget not: in thy book record their groans   5
    Who were thy sheep, and in their ancient fold
    Slain by the bloody Piemontese, that rolled
    Mother with infant down the rocks. Their moans
The vales redoubled to the hills, and they
    To heaven. Their martyred blood and ashes sow   10
    O'er all the Italian fields, where still doth sway
The triple Tyrant; that from these may grow
    A hundredfold, who, having learnt thy way,
    Early may fly the Babylonian woe.

XIX.

ON HIS BLINDNESS.

When I consider how my light is spent
    Ere half my days in this dark world and wide,
    And that one talent which is death to hide
    Lodged with me useless, though my soul more bent
To serve therewith my Maker, and present   5
    My true account, lest He returning chide;
    "Doth God exact day-labour, light denied?"
    I fondly ask. But Patience, to prevent
That murmur, soon replies, "God doth not need
    Either man's work or his own gifts. Who best   10
    Bear his mild yoke, they serve him best. His state
Is kingly: thousands at his bidding speed,
    And post o'er land and ocean without rest;
    They also serve who only stand and wait."

XX.

TO MR. LAWRENCE.

LAWRENCE, of virtuous father virtuous son,
    Now that the fields are dank, and ways are mire,
    Where shall we sometimes meet, and by the fire
    Help waste a sullen day what may be won
From the hard season gaining? Time will run   5
    On smoother, till Favonius reinspire
    The frozen earth, and clothe in fresh attire
    The lily and rose, that neither sowed nor spun.
What neat repast shall feast us, light and choice,
    Of Attic taste, with wine, whence we may rise   10
    To hear the lute well touched, or artful voice
Warble immortal notes and Tuscan air?
    He who of those delights can judge, and spare
    To interpose them oft, is not unwise.

XXI.

TO CYRIACK SKINNER.

CYRIACK, whose grandsire on the royal bench
    Of British Themis, with no mean applause,
    Pronounced, and in his volumes taught, our laws,
    Which others at their bar so often wrench;
To-day deep thoughts resolve with me to drench   5
    In mirth that after no repenting draws;
    Let Euclid rest, and Archimedes pause,
    And what the Swede intends, and what the French.
To measure life learn thou betimes, and know
    Toward solid good what leads the nearest way;   10
    For other things mild Heaven a time ordains,
And disapproves that care, though wise in show,
    That with superfluous burden loads the day,
    And, when God sends a cheerful hour, refrains.

XXII.

TO THE SAME.

CYRIACK, this three years' day these eyes, though clear,
    To outward view, of blemish or of spot,
    Bereft of light, their seeing have forgot;
    Nor to their idle orbs doth sight appear
Of sun, or moon, or star, throughout the year,   5
    Or man, or woman. Yet I argue not
    Against Heaven's hand or will, nor bate a jot
    Of heart or hope, but still bear up and steer
Right onward. What supports me, dost thou ask?
    The conscience, friend, to have lost them overplied   10
    In Liberty's defence, my noble task,
Of which all Europe talks from side to side.
    This thought might lead me through the world's vain mask
    Content, though blind, had I no better guide.

XXIII.

ON HIS DECEASED WIFE.

Methought I saw my late espoused saint
    Brought to me like Alcestis from the grave,
    Whom Jove's great son to her glad husband gave,
    Rescued from Death by force, though pale and faint.
Mine, as whom washed from spot of child-bed taint
    Purification in the Old Law did save,
    And such as yet once more I trust to have
    Full sight of her in Heaven without restraint,
Came vested all in white, pure as her mind.
    Her face was veiled; yet to my fancied sight
    Love, sweetness, goodness, in her person shined
So clear as in no face with more delight.
    But, oh! as to embrace me she inclined,
    I waked, she fled, and day brought back my night.

ON THE NEW FORCERS OF CONSCIENCE UNDER THE LONG PARLIAMENT.

BECAUSE you have thrown off your Prelate Lord,
    And with stiff vows renounced his Liturgy,
    To seize the widowed whore Plurality
    From them whose sin ye envied, not abhorred;
Dare ye for this adjure the civil sword
    To force our consciences that Christ set free,
    And ride with us a classic hierarchy,
    Taught ye by mere A. S. and Rutherford?
Men whose life, learning, faith, and pure intent,
    Would have been held in high esteem with Paul
    Must now be named and printed heretics
By shallow Edwards and Scotch What-d'ye-call!
    But we do hope to find out all your tricks,
    Your plots and packing, worse than those of Trent,
        That so the Parliament
May with their wholesome and preventive shears
Clip your phylacteries, though baulk your ears,
        And succour our just fears,
When they shall read this clearly in your charge:
New "Presbyter" is but old "Priest" writ large.

MILTON! thou shouldst be living at this hour:
England hath need of thee: she is a fen
Of stagnant waters: altar, sword, and pen,
Fireside, the heroic wealth of hall and bower,
Have forfeited their ancient English dower
Of inward happiness. We are selfish men:
Oh! raise us up, return to us again;
And give us manners, virtue, freedom, power.
Thy soul was like a Star, and dwelt apart:
Thou hadst a voice whose sound was like the sea:
Pure as the naked heavens, majestic, free,
So didst thou travel on life's common way,
In cheerful godliness; and yet thy heart
The lowliest duties on herself did lay.—

Wordsworth.

SCORN not the Sonnet; Critic, you have frowned,
Mindless of its just honours; with this key
Shakespeare unlocked his heart; the melody
Of this small lute gave ease to Petrarch's wound;
A thousand times this pipe did Tasso sound;
Camöens soothed with it an exile's grief;
The Sonnet glittered a gay myrtle leaf
Amid the cypress with which Dante crowned
His visionary brow: a glow-worm lamp,
It cheered mild Spenser, called from Faery-land
To struggle through dark ways; and, when a damp
Fell round the path of Milton, in his hand
The Thing became a trumpet, whence he blew
Soul-animating strains—alas, too few!—

Wordsworth.

NOTES.

I.

FIRST printed in 1645; written perhaps about 1630—1631. As Milton placed it first among the Sonnets published in 1645, its composition must have preceded that of the Sonnet "On his being arrived," the probable date of which is December 1631.

The subject of the Sonnet is the old superstition that to hear the nightingale earlier in the year than the cuckoo (which, as a rule, arrives first) portends good fortune in love. Cf. Burton, describing a lover on whom his mistress has smiled favourably, "he is too confident and rapt beyond himself, as if he had heard the Nightingale in the Spring before the Cuckow" (*Anatomy of Melancholy*, vol. II. p. 302, ed. 1800). Milton had read Chaucer's poem *The Cuckow and the Nightingale*; cf. the following stanza:

"But as I lay this other nyght wakynge
I thoght how lovers had a tokenynge,
And among hem hit was a comune tale,
That hit wer good to here the nyghtyngale,
Rather then the leude cukkow synge."

The lover who is supposed to say this goes out in hopes of hearing the nightingale, and does—but not before the note of the cuckoo has surprised him. Then, falling into a kind of 'swoon', he listens to a dialogue between the nightingale and cuckoo, on the "service of Love"; cf. the last couplet of this Sonnet.

Milton seems to have had a peculiar fondness for the nightingale, if we may judge by the number of references to the bird in his poems; cf. *P. L.* III. 38—40, IV. 602, 603, V. 40, 41, VII. 435, 436. See too the lines to the nightingale in *Il Penseroso*, 56—64, a poem written (1632 or 1633) not very long after this Sonnet and descriptive, in great measure, of the poet's own feelings and tastes.

Of the style of the poem Mr Mark Pattison well remarks: "In this sonnet...Milton has not yet shaken himself free from the trick of con-

SONNETS.

triving 'concetti' as was the fashion of the previous age, and especially of his models, the Italians...[Afterwards] his sense of reality asserted itself, and he never again, in the sonnets, lapses into frigid, and far-fetched ingenuities." Of the tendency of Milton's earliest style towards strained and artificial turns of fancy and phrase ('concetti') such as the 'metaphysical' school of poets employed, the *Nativity Hymn* affords striking illustrations; see the Pitt Press edition, *Introduction*, pp. xxvi, xxvii.

1. *nightingale;* literally 'singer by night'; *gale* coming from A. S. *galan*, to sing, akin to *yell*. *spray;* see G.

2. Cf. *P. L.* v. 40, "the night-warbling bird," i.e. the nightingale. *still*, quiet (other birds not singing: cf. *The Merchant of Venice*, v. 104—106). *Still* is a favourite epithet with Milton in his early poems; cf. *Lycidas*, 187, "the still Morn," *Il Penseroso*, 78, 127.

3, 4. The nightingale (a migratory bird) comes to England about the middle of April; hence its note is naturally regarded as heralding spring. Cf. Milton's poem *In Adventum Veris*, 25, 26:

jam, Philomela, tuos, foliis adoperta novellis,
instituis modulos, dum silet omne nemus.

With the last words (*dum silet...*) cf. line 2 of this Sonnet.

4. This allegorical description of the approach of spring is classical. The *Hours*, Lat. *Horæ*, Gk. ὧραι, were goddesses who personified the seasons of the year, the course of which was symbolically called "the dance of the *Horæ*." Cf. *P. L.* IV. 266—268,

"universal Pan,
Knit with the Graces and the *Hours in dance*,
Led on the eternal Spring";

also *P. L.* v. 394, 395, *Comus*, 984—987, and Gray's *Ode to Spring*. *jolly*, see G. *lead on;* the metaphor of a dance.

5. *close*, i.e. with sleep, the Day (personified) being lulled to rest by them. Cf. *Il Penseroso*, 141, "Hide me from Day's garish eye," and *Comus*, 978. Elizabethan writers use "eye of *heaven*"=the sun; cf. Spenser, *Faerie Queene*, I. 3. 4, " As the great eye of heaven shyned bright"; and Shakespeare, Sonnet 18, *King John*, IV. 2. 15.

6. *heard*, if first heard. *shallow*, stupid; referring, perhaps, specially to the bird's stupid, monotonous cry; cf. *Midsummer-Night's Dream*, III. 1. 134, "plain-song cuckoo."

8. Milton elsewhere associates the nightingale with love, speaking of it as "the amorous bird of night" (*P. L.* VIII. 518), and of its song as "love-laboured" (*P. L.* v. 41).

NOTES.   31

9. *timely*, in good time, early. He calls the cuckoo "the rude bird of hate" in allusion to the superstition that its note was unpropitious to lovers, as also to married people; cf. *Midsummer-Night's Dream*, III. 1. 134—139, *Love's Labour's Lost*, V. 2. 908. Mr Mark Pattison cites George Gascoigne: "I have noted as evil luck in love, after the cuckoo's call, to have happened unto divers unmarried folks, as ever I did unto the married." There are many curious beliefs about the cuckoo; see Brand's *Popular Antiquities*, Bohn's ed., II. 197, 198.

11. *too late*, i.e. after he had already heard the cuckoo.

13, 14. Suggested by Chaucer's *The Cuckow and the Nightingale*; the cuckoo sneers at love and the nightingale answers:
"who that wol the god of love not serve,
I dar wel sey he is worthy for to sterve [=die]."
They discuss the point, the nightingale speaking in warm praise "Of Love, and of his worshipful servyse." *Train* ('retinue, followers') is a favourite word with M.; cf. *Il Pen.* 10 ("The fickle pensioners of Morpheus' train"), *S. A.* 721, *P. L.* 1. 478, v. 166 ("Fairest of stars, last in the train of night").

II.

First printed 1645; written just after—perhaps, on—December 9, 1631, Milton's twenty-third birthday. The Sonnet, in his handwriting, occurs in the Cambridge MSS., and there forms part of a letter in prose to one of his friends.

Milton had taken his B.A. degree two years previously and had remained at the University for further study. The unknown friend to whom the letter is addressed (possibly it was never sent) had evidently urged that this period of indefinite study should close, and that Milton should, as the saying is, 'do something'—e.g. carry out his original intention of entering the Church. Milton in reply, while defending study as the means of making him "more fit" for the higher purposes of life, admits that his friend's remonstrance is reasonable: "I am something suspicious of myself, and do take notice of a certain belatedness in me." As a proof, he inserts the Sonnet (composed "some little while ago...in a Petrarchian stanza"), in which he had expressed this feeling of "belatedness" very clearly. Cf. "late spring," l. 4.

The great interest of the poem lies, I think, in its last six lines. The dominating idea of Milton's life was his resolve to use his high gifts for the glory of God, and to achieve this object by writing a great poem. He feels an intense responsibility to do something worthy, and it is revealed plainly in this Sonnet, which has been well called "an inseparable part of Milton's autobiography." See pp. xii, xiii.

3. *career*, speed; this was properly a term of horsemanship=a short gallop at full speed; used especially of tournaments.

4, 5. *shew'th...truth*. For the rhyme, indicating perhaps the pronunciation of *shew* then current, cf. *Comus*, 511, 512:

Spirit. "Ay me unhappy! then my fears are *true*.
Elder Brother. What fears, good Thyrsis? Prithee briefly *shew*."
In *Comus*, 994—996 *hue*, *shew*, *dew* and *true* all rhyme.

5, 6. An allusion to his youthful appearance, which was evidently due, in great measure, to his fresh complexion. Cf. Toland's description of him as "middle sized and well proportioned, his deportment erect and manly, his hair of a light brown, his features exactly regular, his complexion wonderfully fair when a youth, and ruddy to the very last" (*Life* of Milton, 1698). Cf. also Johnson: "Milton has the reputation of having been in his youth eminently beautiful, so as to have been called the lady of his college" (i.e. Christ's College, Cambridge).

Milton himself in 1654, replying to the coarse attacks on his person, writes: "My face...is of a complexion entirely opposite to the pale and cadaverous [as Salmasius had described it]; so that, though I am more than forty years old, there is scarcely any one to whom I do not appear ten years younger than I am," *Second Defence of the People of England*, *P. W.* I. 235, 236. *deceive*, disguise, belie.

8. *timely-happy*, fortunate in reaching early maturity. Cf. his lines on Shakespeare:

"to the shame of slow-endeavouring art
Thy easy numbers flow."

I suppose that he is there, as perhaps here, contrasting himself with Shakespeare, and that the "slow-endeavouring art" is his own.

9. *it*, i.e. "inward ripeness" (7).

10, 11. *even to*, conformable with.

13. *All is*, i.e. "even" (10) already: not merely "shall be" (10).

14. *As ever*, as *being* ever. *Task-Master*; compare *Exodus* i. 11, iii. 7, v. 6, 10.

With these last lines compare Sonnet XIX. (written before *Paradise Lost*), where Milton laments that the "talent" of poetic genius committed to him has not yet been used fully, but that his duty to his "great Task-Master" still remains unfulfilled.

See *Appendix*, I. ("Milton's Great Purpose"), pp. 67—69.

NOTES.

Milton's five Italian Sonnets and the 'Canzone' (which is usually printed with them) were probably written during his stay in Italy 1638—1639. They are rendered thus by Cowper:—

III.

Fair Lady! whose harmonious name the Rhine,
  Through all his grassy vale, delights to hear,
  Base were indeed the wretch, who could forbear
  To love a spirit elegant as thine,
That manifests a sweetness all divine,   5
  Nor knows a thousand winning acts to spare,
  And graces, which Love's bow and arrows are,
  Tempering thy virtues to a softer shine.
When gracefully thou speak'st, or singest gay
  Such strains as might the senseless forest move,   10
  Ah then—turn each his eyes and ears away
Who feels himself unworthy of thy love!
  Grace can alone preserve him, ere the dart
  Of fond desire yet reach his inmost heart.

IV.

As on a hill-top rude, when closing day
  Imbrowns the scene, some pastoral maiden fair
  Waters a lovely foreign plant with care,
  Borne from its native genial airs away,
That scarcely can its tender bud display,   5
  So, on my tongue these accents, new and rare,
  Are flowers exotic, which Love waters there,
  While thus, O sweetly scornful, I essay
Thy praise, in verse to British ears unknown,
  And Thames exchange for Arno's fair domain;   10
  So Love has willed, and ofttimes love has shown
That what he wills, he never wills in vain.
  Oh, that this hard and sterile breast might be
  To him who plants from Heaven a soil as free!

CANZONE.

They mock my toil—the nymphs and amorous swains—
And whence this fond attempt to write, they cry,
Love songs in language that thou little know'st?
How dar'st thou risk to sing these foreign strains?
Say truly. Find'st not oft thy purpose crossed,   5
And that thy fairest flowers here fade and die?
Then with pretence of admiration high—
Thee other shores expect and other tides,
Rivers on whose grassy sides
Her deathless laurel leaf, with which to bind   10
Thy flowing locks, already Fame provides;
Why then this burthen, better far declined?
Speak, Muse, for me.—The fair one said, who guides
My willing heart and all my fancy's flights,
"This is the language in which Love delights."   15

V.

SONNET TO CHARLES DIODATI.

Charles—and I say it wondering—thou must know
  That I, who once assumed a scornful air,
  That scoffed at love, am fallen in his snare
(Full many an upright man has fallen so).
Yet think me not thus dazzled by the flow   5
  Of golden locks, or damask cheek; more rare
  The heart-felt beauties of my foreign fair;
A mien majestic, with dark brows, that show
The tranquil lustre of a lofty mind;
  Words exquisite, of idioms more than one,   10
  And song, whose fascinating power might bind,
And from her sphere draw down the labouring Moon,
  With such fire-darting eyes, that should I fill
  My ears with wax, she would enchant me still.

VI.

Lady, it cannot be, but that thine eyes
  Must be my sun, such radiance they display,
  And strike me even as Phœbus him, whose way
  Through torrid Libya's sandy desert lies.
Meantime, on that side steamy vapours rise   5
  Where most I suffer. Of what kind are they,
  New as to me they are, I cannot say,
  But deem them, in the lover's language—sighs.
Some, though with pain, my bosom close conceals,
  Which, if in part escaping thence, they tend   10
  To soften thine, thy coldness soon congeals.
While others to my tearful eyes ascend,
  Whence my sad nights in showers are ever drowned,
  Till my Aurora comes, her brow with roses bound.

VII.

Enamoured, artless, young, on foreign ground,
  Uncertain whither from myself to fly,
  To thee, dear Lady, with an humble sigh
  Let me devote my heart, which I have found
By certain proofs, not few, intrepid, sound,   5
  Good, and addicted to conceptions high:
  When tempests shake the world, and fire the sky,
  It rests in adamant self-wrapt around,
As safe from envy, and from outrage rude,
  From hopes and fears, that vulgar minds abuse,   10
  As fond of genius and fixed fortitude,
Of the resounding lyre, and every Muse.
  Weak you will find it in one only part,
  Now pierced by Love's immedicable dart.

VIII.

"This Sonnet, the first of those which refer to English public affairs, was written in November 1642, and probably on Saturday the 12th of that month. The Civil War had then begun; and Milton, already known as a vehement Anti-Episcopal pamphleteer [see *Introduction*, p. xv] and Parliamentarian, was living, with two young nephews whom he was educating, in his house in Aldersgate Street, a suburban thoroughfare just beyond one of the city gates of London. After some of the first actions of the war, including the indecisive Battle of Edgehill (Oct. 23), the King's army, advancing out of the Midlands, with the King and Prince Rupert present in it, had come as near to London as Hounslow and Brentford, and was threatening a farther march to crush the Londoners and the Parliament at once. They were at their nearest on Saturday the 12th of November; and all that day and the next there was immense excitement in London in expectation of an assault—chains put up across streets, houses barred, &c. It was not till the evening of the 13th that the citizens were reassured by the retreat of the King's army, which had been checked from a closer advance by a rapid march-out of the Trained Bands under Essex and Skippon. Milton, we are to fancy, had shared the common alarm. His was one of the houses which, if the Cavaliers had been let loose, it would have given them particular pleasure to sack."—*Masson.*

Aldersgate Street where Milton lived was on the way to Islington. It had the great merit, according to Phillips, of being one of the quietest streets in London. Milton refers to his "spacious house" with satisfaction in the *Second Defence* (*P. W.* I. 257).

The heading, "When the assault," in Milton's own writing, is in the Cambridge MS., but not in the editions of 1645, 1673. He crossed out a heading—"On his dore when ye Citty expected an assault."

1. *Colonel*; to be scanned here as 3 syllables. Ital. *colonello*; lit. 'a little column' (*colonna*), i.e. prop, support of the regiment. *Knight in arms*; from *Richard II.* I. 3. 26.

2. i.e. to whom chance may assign the opportunity of seizing.

5—8. This promise of fame conferred by poetry is not, coming from Milton's pen, a mere piece of hackneyed convention; nor has it anything of arrogance. Milton believes in the power which he attributes to poetry (cf. the lines on Shakespeare), and in himself. His greatness has the self-consciousness often allied with real humility and a strong sense of responsibility.

NOTES. 37

5. *charms*, spells, i.e. the magical effect of poetry; see G.

8. *whatever clime*, in every region which. *clime*, see G.

the sun's bright circle; repeated in *P. L.* IV. 578. *circle*, orb, sphere; the 'ball' of the sun, as we say.

10. *Emathian conqueror*, Alexander the Great of Macedonia; lived B.C. 356—323. *Emathia* was "a district of Macedonia...and the original seat of the Macedonian monarchy. The poets frequently give the name of Emathia to the whole of Macedonia" (*Classical Dictionary*). Hence *Emathius* was applied to Alexander; cf. Ovid's *Tristia*, III. 5. 39, *ducis Emathii clementia*. See *P. R.* III. 290, where Milton speaks of the great Seleucia as "built by Emathian...hands," because founded by Alexander's Macedonian general, Seleucus. Other allusions to Alexander occur in *P. R.* II. 196—198, III. 31—34.

10—12. According to the story told by Pliny, *Natural History*, VII. 29, and by other writers, when Alexander captured Thebes in B.C. 333 and sacked the city, he ordered that the house of the poet Pindar (lived B.C. 522—442) should be spared.

Cf. the *Glosse* to Spenser's *Shepheards Calender, October:* "Alexander destroying Thebes, when he was enformed, that the famous Lyrick poet Pindarus was borne in that citie, not onely commaunded streightly, that no man should, upon payne of death, do any violence to that house, by fire or otherwise: but also specially spared most, and some highly rewarded, that were of hys kinne."

The chief patrons of Pindar, who spent most of his life at Thebes, were Alexander of Macedonia, an ancestor of Alexander the Great, and Hieron of Syracuse; "and the praises which he bestowed upon the former are said to have been the chief reason which led his descendant Alexander [the Great] to spare the house of the poet, when he destroyed the rest of Thebes"—*Classical Dictionary*. Alexander had been sent in his youth to Athens to study in the school (*Lyceum*) of Aristotle (cf. *P. R.* IV. 251—253); hence he had much sympathy with Greek culture.

For interesting allusions in Milton to Pindar's works see *P. R.* IV. 256, 257; the sixth *Elegy*, 23—26; *Church Government*, Preface to bk. II., *P. W.* II. 479. See also *Appendix*, II., pp. 69, 70.

12—14. "Plutarch relates, that when the Lacedæmonian general Lysander took Athens [B.C. 404], it was proposed in a council of war entirely to raze the city, and convert its site into a desert." But while the matter was still undecided, "at a banquet of the chief officers, a certain Phocian sang some fine [verses] from a chorus of the *Electra* of

Euripides; which so affected the hearers, that they declared it an unworthy act to reduce a place, so celebrated for the production of illustrious men, to total ruin and desolation. It appears, however, that Lysander ordered the walls and fortifications to be demolished"—*Warton*. The verses in question were part of the first chorus of the *Electra*, 167 *et seq.*

Speaking of Milton's learning, Johnson says: "The books in which his daughter, who used to read to him, represented him as most delighting, after Homer, which he could almost repeat, were Ovid's 'Metamorphoses' and Euripides" (*Life* of Milton). A copy of Euripides with MS. notes by Milton is extant, and one of his textual emendations —ἡδέως for ἡδέων in the *Bacchæ*, 188—is universally adopted. See Dr Sandys's edition of the *Bacchæ* (Cambridge Press), where in the notes on 188, 234—236 and 314—318 several interesting parallels between *Comus* and parts of Euripides are pointed out.

Noticeable allusions to Euripides occur in *Church Government* (*P. W.* II. 479), *On Education* (*P. W.* III. 472, 473), and the *Preface* to *Samson Agonistes* (lines 58, 59). See too Sonnet XXIII., and p. 69.

12. *repeated*, recited.

13. *sad;* probably it qualifies *Electra*, the point of the epithet being explained by the play *Electra*. But some refer it to "poet," with the common Miltonic sense 'grave, serious.'

IX.

Printed 1645; written about 1643-44. The lady may have been a Miss Davis, with whom M. was very friendly (Mark Pattison).

"In the Cambridge MS. we find that Milton had originally written '*blooming virtue*' for '*growing virtues*' in line 7, and that line 13 ran originally thus:

'*Opens the door of bliss that hour of night.*'

Both passages are corrected into their present form on the margin"—*Masson*.

2. Cf. *Matthew* vii. 13, 14: "Broad is the way, that leadeth to destruction,...and narrow is the way, which leadeth unto life."

the green; i.e. a soft way through grassy, pleasant places, not the hard, rough highway; cf. Shakespeare's phrase "the primrose path," *Hamlet*, I. 3. 50 (varied in *Macbeth*, II. 3. 21). Symbolism of this kind is quite in Milton's style.

NOTES. 39

We have a similar figurative idea in *P. R.* I. 478, "Hard are the ways of truth, and rough to walk."

4. *the hill of Truth*. Suggested by the allegory, as old as the *Works and Days*, 287 *et seq.* of Hesiod (8th century B.C.), that Virtue dwells on a hill steep and difficult of ascent. Cf. *P. R.* II. 217, "Seated as on the top of Virtue's hill." In one of his letters Milton speaks of "that steep and rugged way which leads to the pinnacle of Virtue." *The Faerie Queene* is full of such allegory, e. g. the Hill of Contemplation (I. 10).

5. Cf. *Luke* x. 42, "Mary hath chosen that good part"; and *Ruth* i. 14—17.

7, 8. *spleen*, ill temper, malice. *ruth*, compassion; see G.

10—14. See the parable of the Virgins, *Matthew* xxv.

11. "Hope maketh not ashamed," *Romans* v. 5.

12. Cf. *Samson Agonistes*, 1741, "on feastful days"; i.e. 'feast-days,' as we say. So "feastfull glee," *The Faerie Queene*, VI. 10. 22.

13. *hour;* changed in the Cambridge MS. from *watch*.

X.

Written probably 1643 or 1644; the last of the Sonnets printed in the edition of 1645. It is among the Cambridge MSS.

The "good Earl" whose merits the Sonnet celebrates was James Ley, first Earl of Marlborough; a Judge and politician of some distinction. Born in 1550, the son of a Devonshire gentleman, he rose to various high offices of the law; later, became Lord High Treasurer, 1624, and was made a Baron—afterwards, 1626, an Earl. Resigning the Treasury in 1628, he held for a few months the post of President of the Council. He retired from office altogether at the end of 1628 and died on March 14, 1629, four days after the dissolution of Charles's third Parliament. Milton implies that the event hastened the Earl's death. The two highest offices to which he attained are skilfully referred to (1—4); perhaps, with the implication that he resigned rather than be a party to the king's unconstitutional methods.

His daughter Lady Margaret married a Captain Hobson from the Isle of Wight; at the time when this Sonnet was written they were living in London. Milton's wife had returned to her father's house (see *Introduction*, p. xvi.), and, says Phillips, "Our author, now as it were a single man again, made it his chief diversion, now and then in an evening to visit the Lady Margaret Ley. This lady being a woman of great wit and ingenuity, had a particular honour for

40   SONNETS.

him and took much delight in his company, as likewise her husband Captain Hobson, a very accomplished gentleman; and what esteem he [Milton] at the same time had for her appears by a Sonnet he made in praise of her" (*Life* of Milton, 1694).

1. Note repetition (1, 5, 6, 8) of *that*='the well-known' (Lat. *ille*).
4. *more in himself content*, preferring a private station.
5, 6. *breaking*, failure; or 'breaking up,' dissolution. *broke,* broke down. M., like Shakespeare, uses word-plays to express bitterness.
6. *dishonest*=Lat. *inhonestus*, disgraceful, i.e. to those who won the victory: an *oxymoron*. "Inglorious triumphs and dishonest scars" (Pope).
7. *Chæronea*; a town in Bœotia; the scene of the defeat of the united army of the Athenians and Bœotians by Philip of Macedon in August, 338 B.C. This battle finally put an end to the independence of Greece: hence the 'dishonour,' Milton says, of winning it.
8. The allusion is to Isocrates, one of the greatest of Athenian orators. "Although Isocrates took no part in public affairs, he was an ardent lover of his country; and, accordingly, when the battle of Chæronea had destroyed the last hopes of freedom, he put an end to his life, B.C. 338, at the age of 98"—*Classical Dictionary*. But this tradition of his suicide does not rest on very sound evidence, according to Professor Jebb.

The title of Milton's *Areopagitica* is adapted from the λόγος Ἀρεοπαγιτικός, 'Areopagitic Discourse,' of Isocrates, who is referred to at the outset of the work, and again in *On Education* (cf. "those ancient and famous schools of Pythagoras, Plato, *Isocrates*, Aristotle"); see *P. W.* II. 52, III. 474. A small portion of the orations of Isocrates is extant.

old man eloquent. This order of words—a noun placed between two qualifying words—is frequent in Milton's works. Cf. "sad occasion dear," *Lycidas*, 6; "towered structure high," *P. L.* I. 733. We find it in Greek; cf. Euripides, *Phœnissae*, 234, "νιφόβολον ὄρος ἱρόν." Gray probably imitated Milton; cf. his *Elegy*, 53, "Full many a gem of purest ray serene." There are instances in Tennyson's early poems (which reveal Milton's influence constantly). See Sonnet XVIII. 2.

9, 10. Not to be taken too literally. Milton means that he (born 1608) was a mere child when the Earl was in his prime ("flourished") and rising to high offices.

to have known. Elizabethan writers use the perfect infinitive to express something that might have been but was not, especially with verbs of hoping, intending—e.g. "He trusted to have equalled the Most High," *P. L.* I. 40. See Abbott, *Shakesp. Grammar*, p. 259.

XI.

"The heading was first prefixed to the following Sonnet, which was originally numbered 11....In ed. 1673 the order of Sonnets XI. and XII. was changed to the present. The first draft [in the Cambridge MS.] is in Milton's own hand, and there is a fair copy by another"—*Aldis Wright.*

First printed 1673; written probably about the middle of 1645, as the *Tetrachordon*, "writ of *late*," was published in March of that year.

The original draft of the Sonnet differs in several lines from the published version, the alterations being shown in the Cambridge MS. Thus in l. 10 *rugged* was substituted for *rough-hewn* (cf. *Hamlet*, V. 2. 11), while *rough-hewn* had been substituted for *barbarous*.

Milton's *Doctrine and Discipline of Divorce*, his first pamphlet on the subject and the immediate outcome of his unhappy marriage, appeared in 1643. The unusual views expressed in it gave great offence, to Presbyterians and Puritans in general no less than to Episcopalians. In reply to his critics Milton published several treatises enforcing his views; among them was the *Tetrachordon* (1645). Its name, from Gk. τετράχορδος, '*four*-stringed,' was explained on the title-page, which described the work as "Expositions upon the *four* chief places in Scripture which treat of marriage, or nullities in marriage." The texts expounded are *Genesis* i. 27, 28 (taken in conjunction with *Genesis* ii. 18, 23, 24); *Deuteronomy* xxiv. 1, 2; *Matthew* v. 31, 32 (taken in conjunction with chapter xix. 3—11); and 1 *Corinthians* vii. 10—16.

In his *Second Defence* Milton says that one reason why he published these works advocating greater freedom of divorce was the divided state of the nation, it being often the case that husband and wife took different sides in the Revolution (*P. W.* I. 259). His own wife belonged to a Royalist family.

3. *walked the town*, i.e. was circulated. *the town* = London.

4. *good intellects.* It was ever Milton's claim that he appealed to "*fit* audience, though few" (*P. L.* VII. 31).

7, 8. *Mile-End Green;* "so called from its distance, roughly measured, from the central parts of London: it was a common in Milton's time, and the favourite terminus of a citizen's walk"—*Masson.* Now it is part of Whitechapel.

8, 9. Milton chooses Scotch names in sarcastic allusion to the Presbyterians (mostly Scotch) who had condemned his opinions on divorce, and were evidently becoming almost as distasteful to him (see pp. 60—63) as the Episcopal followers of Laud had been. These particular Scotch names must often have been on the lips of Londoners at the time when this Sonnet was probably written—viz. the middle of 1645—as they were associated with the campaign of Montrose, who in the summer of 1645 was at the height of his success.

"Among Montrose's most influential adherents in his enterprise there were several *Gordons*, of whom the most prominent were George, Lord Gordon, the eldest son of the Marquis of Huntly, and his next brother Charles Gordon, Viscount Aboyne"—*Masson*.

According to Dr Masson, the three names in line 9 all belonged to the same person, viz. "Alexander Macdonald the younger," usually called "Young *Colkitto*" (='left-handed'); one of the chief officers of Montrose. See the description in Scott's *Legend of Montrose*, xv.

10. *like*, i.e. rugged like the names. Dr Bradshaw explains "mouths such as ours; our-like." *sleek*, smooth because familiar.

11. *Quintilian;* the celebrated Roman critic and rhetorician; lived A.D. 40—118. Milton refers to Quintilian's great work, the treatise on rhetoric (*De Institutione Oratoria Libri* XII.), in *On Education*, *P. W.* III. 468.

12, 13. The sense is—Thy age did not hate learning worse than a toad, as our age does: *then* a Greek title like *Tetrachordon* would not have been so misunderstood or criticised as it is now. It was, I daresay, to show his contempt for his critics that he called his next pamphlet on divorce by a similar Greek name, viz. *Colasterion*, = Gk. κολαστήριον, 'an instrument of correction,' from κολάζειν, 'to chastise, correct.' Cf. too the title of the *Areopagitica*.

12. *Sir John Cheke;* lived 1514—1557; first holder of the Professorship of Greek at Cambridge established by Henry VIII. in 1540 (but Erasmus had lectured there previously—cf. Gibbon's famous sarcasm); and afterwards tutor to Edward VI.

Milton refers to Cheke not merely because he was a famous Greek scholar, but because (as Masson notes) he had been a member of the Commission appointed by Edward VI. in 1549 to formulate a code of ecclesiastical law in place of the old canon law. This Commission, of which Cranmer was the head, proposed certain relaxations of the existing Church-laws of divorce. Milton refers to it at the end of *Tetrachordon* and says that the carrying out of its proposals was only prevented by the untimely death of the king. He mentions the names of some of the Commissioners—among them "Sir John Cheke, *the king's tutor*, a man at that time counted the learnedest of Englishmen, and for piety not inferior" (*P. W.* III. 432).

13. *Hated not learning.* He has in mind the great expansion of

NOTES. 43

learning in the 16th century (especially seen in the revived study of Greek) which was part of the Renaissance.

13. *asp;* see G. and cf. *P. L.* x. 524.

14. *taught'st Cambridge.* Among Cheke's pupils at St John's College were William Cecil (afterwards Lord Burghley) and Roger Ascham, who speaks of Cheke with admiration several times in his *Toxophilus* and in *The Schoolmaster* (see Arber's ed., pp. 67, 154, with the editor's *Introduction*, pp. 6, 7).

Cheke's tenure of the Professorship was notable for the controversy as to the pronunciation of Greek. The comparatively few Englishmen who then knew Greek pronounced it very much in the way that continental Scholars now pronounce it. Cheke introduced at Cambridge a pronunciation similar to that now current in England. Stephen Gardiner, the Chancellor of the University, endeavoured to stop the innovation.

and King Edward. Cheke also acted sometimes as tutor to the Princess (afterwards Queen) Elizabeth.

XII.

A continuation of the subject. See first note on Sonnet XI.

1. *clogs*, restraints; literally 'encumbrances' such as are put upon animals to prevent them straying; an appropriate word therefore in view of the latter part of line 4.

4. *cuckoos;* see Sonnet I. 6. A term of contempt, as now, in *2 Henry IV.* II. 4. 387. M. first wrote *buzzards*; an *inferior* kind of hawk—hence meant contemptuously.

5—7. *twinborn progeny;* Apollo and Artemis (=Diana in Roman mythology); god and goddess of the sun and moon respectively.

Ovid tells the story that soon after their birth their mother the goddess Latona (or Leto), while wandering in Lycia, sought to drink from a pool, but was prevented by Lycian peasants ("hinds") who threatened and "railed" at her (*minas...conviciaque insuper addunt*): whereupon she changed them all into frogs, which even *sub aqua maledicere tentant.* See the *Metamorphoses* VI. 339—381.

7. *in fee*, in possession, 'as their own'; see G. The line "intimates the good hopes which Milton had of himself, and his expectations of making a considerable figure in the world"—*Newton.*

8. *Matthew* vii. 6. In the same contemptuous spirit that inspired

44 SONNETS.

this verse he placed on the title-page of *Tetrachordon* these lines (299—302) from the *Medea* of his favourite Euripides:

σκαιοῖσι μὲν γὰρ καινὰ προσφέρων σοφὰ
δόξεις ἀχρεῖος κοὐ σοφὸς πεφυκέναι·
τῶν δ' αὖ δοκούντων εἰδέναι τι ποικίλον
κρείσσων νομισθεὶς λυπρὸς ἐν πόλει φανεῖ.

10. *still*, always, ever. "The truth shall make you free," *John* viii. 32.

11, 12. A favourite sentiment of Milton. Cf. his *Tenure of Kings*, "indeed, none can love freedom heartily but good men; the rest love not freedom but licence," *P. W.* II. 2. So in the *Second Defence* he says that only virtuous men can retain liberty after it is won, *P. W.* I. 295. Love of liberty was one of the ruling impulses of Milton's own life. Every one of his pamphlets was "written on the side of liberty"— Mark Pattison. (See notes on *P. L.* II. 255—277, XI. 798, 799, *Samson Agonistes*, 268—271, Pitt Press editions.)

14. *For all*, in spite of all. *waste...loss*, i.e. in the Civil War.

XIII.

Written, as we learn from the Cambridge MS., in February 1646. First printed 1648, being prefixed to a volume of "Choice Psalmes, put into Musick for three Voices: composed by Henry and William Lawes, Brothers, and Servants to his Majestie: 1648." Henry Lawes, 1595—1662, a "Gentleman of the Chapel Royal" (i.e. one of the royal choir), and a member of the king's "private music" (orchestra), was the chief composer of his age. He was specially noted as a composer of incidental music for Masques and of songs. He wrote the music for *Comus* (and probably for *Arcades*), acted the part of "the Attendant Spirit" when the piece was first performed at Ludlow Castle in 1634, and was responsible for the publication of the first edition in 1637. He seems to have been one of Milton's earliest and most intimate friends, thanks, no doubt, to their common love of music. At the time when this Sonnet was written their intimacy had evidently not been affected by political differences, though Lawes, like his brother (who fell fighting for the king at Chester in 1645), was an ardent Royalist, and the volume of *Psalms* to which Milton's poem was prefixed was dedicated to Charles. After 1648 we do not hear of Lawes in connection with Milton, so that the force of circumstances may have driven them apart. (See *Introductions* to *Arcades and*

Comus, Pitt Press edition; also the Article on Lawes in Grove's *Dictionary of Music*.)

1—4. A very precise and musicianly description of Lawes's songs. He was content to make his music subordinate to the words, preserving their rhythm and accent with fidelity; so that the poetry, not the music (very often, a kind of recitative), was the chief element. This quality explains his great popularity with the poets of the period, many of whom, e.g. Herrick, Cartwright, and Waller, had songs set to music by him. See *Appendix*, III. ("Milton and Music"), pp. 71, 72.

3. *just note and accent*. Cf. the preface on "The Verse" of *Paradise Lost*, where Milton says that one of the main elements of "true musical delight" in poetry is "fit quantity of syllables": by which he means, I think, that each stress or accent should fall naturally, i.e. that a syllable should not be forced by exigence of the metre to bear an accent alien to it. *just*, exact, proper (Lat. *justus*).

4. *Midas*, king of Phrygia. "Once when Pan and Apollo were engaged in a musical contest on the flute and lyre, Midas was chosen to decide between them. The king decided in favour of Pan, whereupon Apollo *changed his ears into those of an ass*"—*Classical Dictionary*.

committing, matching, pairing; cf. Lat. *committere*, used of matching combatants. Milton wrote *misjoining* and then changed.

5, 7. Newton quotes Horace's *Odes: secernunt populo* (I. 1. 32)—cf. "exempts thee from the throng" (=gives you a place apart from ordinary musicians); and *scriberis Vario fortis et hostium | victor* (1. 6. 1).

exempts; a singular verb following *two* nouns which really form *one* idea is common in Elizabethan poetry; cf. *Lycidas*, 6, 7.

6. Milton first wrote "And gives thee praise above the pipe of Pan," by which perhaps he intended to contrast Pan with Apollo (cf. "Phœbus," 10), i.e. *to* continue the classical allusion suggested in line 4.

wan; as we say, '*pale* with envy.'

8. *smooth air*. Cf. *Comus*, 86, where Milton speaks of the "smooth-dittied song" of Thyrsis—an obvious compliment to Lawes who took the part of Thyrsis (i.e. the "Attendant Spirit"). See also *Comus*, 494—496 (with note).

9. *lend;* so the Cambridge MS.; the 1673 edition has *send*, which seems to be a misprint. Newton first adopted *lend*.

10. *Phœbus' quire*, the poets of the time. *quire*, see G.

11. *hymn*, i.e. sacred compositions such as the *Choice Psalmes* mentioned already, and the Coronation-anthem, "Zadock the Priest,"

written for the accession of Charles II. Lawes, however, was not one of our great Church-composers.

story. A marginal note to the Sonnet as first published (1648) explains that this alludes to "The Story of Ariadne set by him [i.e. Lawes] to music." One of the airs for this *Complaint of Ariadne* (so the 'Story' was entitled) gained such celebrity at the time that Milton's allusion was very apposite. The *Complaint* was by Cartwright, a minor poet and dramatist, for many of whose poems Lawes composed music. (Partly from Warton's note.)

12—14. The allusion is to Dante's *Purgatorio* (wherein the poet imagines himself to visit Purgatory), II. 10. Cf. Warton's note: "Dante, on his arrival in Purgatory, sees a vessel approaching the shore, freighted with souls under the conduct of an angel, to be cleansed from their sins and made fit for Paradise. When they are disembarked the poet recognises in the crowd his old friend Casella, the musician. In the course of an affectionate dialogue, the poet requests a soothing air; and Casella sings Dante's second canzone [in the] *Convito*....The Italian commentators say that Casella, Dante's friend, was a musician of distinguished excellence. He must have died a little before the year 1300."

The following is from Mr A. J. Butler's version of the *Purgatorio*; Dante addresses Casella : "'If a new law takes not away from thee memory or use in the amorous chant which was wont to quiet all my wishes, let it please thee therewith to comfort somewhat my soul, which coming here with its body is so wearied.' *Love, which discourses in my mind to me*, then began he so sweetly, that the sweetness yet sounds within me. My Master [Vergil], and I, and that folk who were with him appeared so content, as though naught else touched the minds of any. We were all fixed and intent on his notes."

"A ballad set to music by Casella is said to be still extant in the Vatican Library."—*A. J. Butler*.

12, 13. Originally these lines ran thus in the Cambridge MS.:
"Fame, by the Tuscan's leave, shall set thee higher
Than old Casell, whom Dante won to sing."

Dante was a native of Florence, the capital of Tuscany. The influence of his works on Milton is seen clearly in *Paradise Lost*. In a letter from Florence, September 1638, Milton speaks of himself "retiring with avidity and delight to feast on Dante, Petrarch," *P. W.* III. 497.

14. *milder*, i.e. less terrible than those of Hell, which Dante described in his earlier poem the *Inferno*.

XIV.

First printed 1673. The heading of this Sonnet in the Cambridge MS. (which shows that Milton made a number of changes in the original draft) fixes its date of composition, 1646. Three or four years later Milton lived near Charing Cross at the house of a Mr Thomson; perhaps "Mrs Catherine Thomson" belonged to the same family— *Newton*. The Sonnet is entitled "An Elegy" in an early (1713) ed.

3. *earthy;* so the edition of 1673; now sometimes misprinted *earthly*. Cf. "this earthy grossness," *On Time*, 20.

4. Cf. *Samson Agonistes*, 100, "To live a life half dead, a living death"; Hall's *Satires* V. 2, "And each day dying lives, and living dies."

6. *nor in the grave,* i.e. were not buried with thee, as if done with.

7. *golden rod;* suggested perhaps by *Revelation* xxi. 15.

8. Cf. *Paradise Lost*, XI. 43, XII. 549—551.

10. Cf. *Comus*, 782, "the sun-clad power of chastity," and *On Time*, 21, "attired with stars." The idea may be from *Revelation* xii. 1. *purple;* see G.

14. "Thou shalt make them drink of the river of thy pleasures," *Psalm* xxxvi. 8. See also *Revelation* vii. 17, xxii. 1, to which there are similar allusions in *Par. Lost*, III. 358, 359, V. 652, XI. 78, 79, *Lycidas*, 174, *Epitaphium Damonis*, 206, 207.

thy fill; now a somewhat vulgar expression, but not then; cf. *Leviticus* xxv. 19, *Deuteronomy* xxiii. 24. So in *Par. Lost*, V. 504.

immortal; cf. "*living* fountains," "water of *life*" in *Revelation*.

XV.

Sonnets XV, XVI, XVII. A group of kindred, political Sonnets.

This and the following Sonnet were not printed in the edition of 1673, on acount of their political tone. They first appeared, with numerous imperfections of text, in the *Life* of Milton by his nephew Phillips, 1694. Fortunately both are in the Cambridge MS., the text of which is followed by modern editors. Bishop Newton first transcribed them from the MS.

The Sonnet was written in 1648, between June 13, when Fairfax laid siege to Colchester, and August 17, when Cromwell defeated the Scottish army; see note on line 8. In 1648 the Royalists made a fresh and final effort. There were "new rebellions" (line 6) in the king's behalf in Kent, the west of England and Wales, and Scotland sent an army to his aid. Defeated by Fairfax at Maidstone, the surviving leaders of the Royalists in the east retreated to Colchester, which was besieged from June 13 to August 27. This poem therefore was prompted by, and surely breathes the spirit of, a national crisis.

It is addressed to the Commander-in-chief of the Parliamentary forces —Thomas, the third Lord Fairfax; born 1612, died 1671. Milton and he were contemporaries at Cambridge, Fairfax being of St John's Coll.

2. *envy*, slighting, depreciatory remarks; rather than *envious* in modern sense.

4. *that daunt remotest kings*, i.e. with the fear that their monarchies like the English would be overthrown.

5. *virtue=valour* (which Phillips's edition reads); for this Latin use (=*virtus*) see G. and cf. *Par. Lost*, I. 319, 320:

"After the toil of battle to repose
Your wearied virtue."

Fairfax was distinguished by extreme personal courage; several of his contemporaries make mention of it; Cromwell (*Letter* XXIX) specially commended his bravery at the battle of Naseby. Compare too Milton's words in the *Second Defence*, where, enumerating the great leaders on the side of the Commonwealth, he says: "Nor would it be right to pass over the name of Fairfax, who united the utmost fortitude with the utmost courage; and the spotless innocence of whose life seemed to point him out as the peculiar favourite of Heaven," *P. W.* I. 286, 287.

7. Cf. 1 *Henry IV.*, V. 4. 25, "Another king! they grow like Hydra's heads," and *Henry V.*, I. 1. 35, "Hydra-headed wilfulness." The allusion is to the Lernean Hydra, a nine-headed serpent or 'dragon.' To slay it was one of the 'labours' of Hercules. When he cut off one head two fresh ones came in its stead. Similarly, Milton implies that as one Royalist uprising in one part of England was crushed by the Parliament, another began elsewhere.

8. *league*, i.e. the Solemn League and Covenant between the Parliament and the Scots, 1643. At the time when these lines were written the Scottish army under Hamilton was invading England in support of Charles: hence Milton says "*false* North," "*broken* league."

serpent wings. "Euripides, Milton's favourite, is the only writer of antiquity that has given wings to the monster Hydra"—*Warton.* Cf. the description of the Hydra in the *Ion* 195, where, however, instead of πτανόν, 'winged,' some editors would read πανόν, 'torch.' Several of the offspring of the half-serpent Echidna, mother of the Hydra, were winged monsters, e.g. the Sphinx and the Gorgon, so that the attribution of wings to the Hydra is not so strange. Moreover winged 'dragons' are often mentioned in ancient writers; see *Par. Lost*, VII. 484, note.

imp, repair; see G. *their*, i.e. of the "new rebellions" (6).

12—14. More than once in his prose-works Milton makes it plain that the Civil troubles led to much jobbery and malpractice, the baser Parliamentarians using their power as a means of self-aggrandizement, enrichment, and personal revenge. See *Second Defence, P. W.* I. 297. It was his boast that he himself had been ruined rather than enriched; see *Samson Agonistes*, 697, note. *fraud*, general dishonesty.

XVI.

First printed (like the preceding Sonnet) by Phillips in 1694; in a form differing considerably, and for the worse, from the version in the Cambridge MS., which is now followed by all editors. Written probably in May 1652.

The Sonnet has an obvious affinity to that addressed to Fairfax, being equally the outcome of a crisis (as Milton thought) in the nation's history. It is not, Masson remarks, a general expression of Milton's admiration for Cromwell, but a special appeal invoked by certain circumstances. That appeal comes in the last four lines and is the climax to which the preceding ten lines have led up; its nature is indicated by the title of the Sonnet.

"*The committee for the propagation of the gospel* was a committee of the Rump Parliament. It consisted of fourteen members, and had general administrative duties in church affairs, specially that of supplying spiritual destitution in the parishes. The *proposals of certain ministers* were fifteen proposals offered to the committee by John Owen, and other well-known ministers, in which they asked that the preachers should receive a public maintenance."—*Mark Pattison*.

1. *Cromwell*. The best commentary on the historical aspect of the earlier part of the poem, and on Milton's feelings towards Cromwell, is the long passage in the *Second Defence* (1654) in which the character and services of the Protector are reviewed eulogistically, and his responsibilities to the nation discussed, *P. W.* I. 282—291. Whether Milton

was brought into personal contact with Cromwell has been doubted.

1, 2. *cloud...of war;* Vergil's phrase *nubes belli—Æneid,* X. 809.

2. *detractions;* contrasted with "truth" (4); he refers, perhaps, mainly to the Presbyterians. Cf. the *Second Defence* (1654), "The Presbyterians and the enemy [i.e. the Royalists] impute every harsh treatment which they experience not to the Parliament but to Cromwell alone...against him every invective is levelled, and every censure passed," *P. W.* I. 283.

5. *on the neck;* cf. *Joshua* x. 24, "Come near, put your feet upon the necks of these kings": an obvious symbol of triumphing over.

crowned Fortune proud; for the order see Sonnet X. 8, note.

6. *reared,* raised, set up. *pursued,* followed up steadily.

7—9. The victorious battles of Cromwell alluded to are: Preston, August 17, 1648, when he defeated the Scots under Hamilton; Dunbar, Sept. 3, 1650, a complete rout of the Scottish army under David Leslie; and Worcester, Sept. 3, 1651. All three battles are mentioned in the *Second Defence, P. W.* I. 284, 287, 288.

7. *Darwen;* a stream which runs into the Ribble near Preston.

9. Elizabethan poets were fond of the phrase "wreath of victory"; cf. *Julius Cæsar,* V. 3. 82, "Put on my brows this wreath of victory."

10, 11. One of the not many familiar quotations from Milton.

11—14. The practical object of the proposals against which Milton protests was to establish a Presbyterian Church supported by the State. Milton's objection was twofold : (1) that there ought to be no union of secular and spiritual matters—cf. the antithesis in line 12 between "soul" and "secular"; (2) that ministers of religion, if remunerated at all, should receive only the voluntary offerings of their congregations. This objection to a paid ("hireling") ministry occurs constantly in his works; see *Lycidas,* 118—131, *Par. Lost,* IV. 192, 193, XII. 508—511, with notes. In *Christian Doctrine,* I. XXXI, he deals with the subject at some length, arguing that ministers might support themselves "by the exercise of some calling, by some industry," and so not need remuneration for their ministry ; or failing this, that "they should look for the necessary support of life, not from the edicts of the civil power, but from the spontaneous goodwill and liberality of the church in requital of their voluntary service." He was especially bitter against the Presbyterian ministers, denouncing them for greed in his last pamphlet on religion, *The Likeliest Means to Remove Hirelings out of the Church* (1659), and in other treatises. See *P. W.* II. 36, III. 18, 19, IV. 460; and *Appendix,* IV., V., pp. 72—74.

NOTES.

13, 14. The only rhymed couplet at the end of one of Milton's Sonnets. *free;* see "On The New Forcers of Conscience," 6.

14. *wolves.* See the parable of the 'Good Shepherd,' *John* x. 12; and *Acts* xx. 29. With Milton it is a favourite metaphor for avaricious ministers of religion; cf. *Par. Lost*, XII. 508—511:

"Wolves shall succeed for teachers, grievous wolves,
Who all the sacred mysteries of Heaven
To their own vile advantages shall turn
Of *lucre* and ambition."

See *P. W.* II. 36, IV. 460.

maw, stomach, Germ. *magen;* a vulgar word used more of animals than of men. Perhaps M. had in mind *Philippians* iii. 19: "Whose end is destruction, whose God is their belly."

XVII.

First printed in the *Life and Death of Sir H. Vane* by George Sikes, 1662, with the date of its composition, July 3, 1652. This date, coupled with the fact that Vane was the leader of the Independents, and so opposed to the Presbyterians, links the Sonnet with that to Cromwell. It is among the Cambridge MSS.

"Sir Henry Vane The Younger"; born 1612; Governor of Massachusetts, 1636, 1637; afterwards one of the most prominent members of the Long Parliament and chief opponents of the king; a leading Independent and Republican; excluded at the Restoration from the Act of Indemnity and, after an unjust trial, executed on June 14, 1662. Milton alludes to his fate in *Samson Agonistes*, 692—696. Called "the Younger" to distinguish him from his father, also Sir Henry Vane.

1, 2. *young*, i.e. then about forty. *than whom.* Dr Bradshaw notes that M. has this phrase in *P. L.* I. 490, II. 299, V. 805. After the relative, but only then, it is customary to use the objective case (*whom*) with *than*. Strictly the use, which makes *than* a preposition, is not defensible. See West's *Elements of English Grammar*, p. 257.

3. *gowns, not arms.* The common antithesis between *togæ* and *arma* (i.e. the civil power and the military), as in *cedant arma togæ*.

4. *The fierce Epirot;* Pyrrhus, king of Epirus; born 318 B.C., died 272. His first invasion of Italy was in 280—278, his second in 276—275. *Epirot* = ἠπειρώτης, a native of ἤπειρος, 'mainland,' the name of a country (modern Albania) on the north-west coast of Greece.

the African bold; Hannibal, the great Carthaginian general (see *P. R.* III. 35); born 247 B.C., died about 183. He invaded Italy 218, and was not driven out till 203. Historically it is true that the failure of Pyrrhus and Hannibal was due as much to the administration and diplomacy ("gowns") of the Roman Senate as to the army ("arms").

6. i.e. the perplexing policy of deceptive states. Probably he means the Dutch, against whom war was declared during that very month (July). *spelled*, understood, read aright.

7—9. Vane had been appointed treasurer of the navy by Charles in 1637, and by the Parliament on the outbreak of the Civil War; and in 1642 was a member of the Parliament's committee of defence. A few months after this Sonnet was written he was made chairman of the commission for managing the affairs of the army and navy, and it was mainly through his energy and skill in organising that the fleet with which Blake defeated Van Tromp, in 1653, was fitted out. In 1659 Vane was again the chairman of a similar commission. His administrative capacity in such matters was evidently of a high order—as Milton implies.

7, 8. The saying that money is 'the sinews of war,' i.e. the main strength of, was proverbial in classical writers; Cicero has it, *Philippics* 5. 2 (*nervi belli pecunia*). For *nerve* (Lat. *nervus*, 'sinew'), used in this metaphorical sense='strength, chief support of,' cf. *Troilus and Cressida*, I. 3. 55, "Thou great commander, nerve and bone of Greece."

10, 11. We have noticed already Milton's feeling with regard to the severance of the spiritual and secular powers; see Sonnet XVI. 11—14, note. He wrote a tract *Of Civil Power in Ecclesiastical Causes.*

thou hast learned; by practical experience, as Governor of Massa-chusetts: a post in which Vane had shown great capacity.

12. *The bounds of either sword*, the limits of each power; for the sword as a symbol of authority, cf. 'the sword of justice.' See also *On the New Forcers of Conscience*, 5.

14. *eldest son*, i.e. chief supporter.

XVIII.

This Sonnet was evoked by the sufferings in 1655 of the Waldenses or Vaudois, a sect which appears to have originated about the close of the 12th century. In the first instance, they were the followers of a Lyons merchant Peter Waldo (cf. their original name Waldenses),

NOTES. 53

whose teaching anticipated the Protestant principles of the Reformation. As, with increasing numbers, the sect became more important, they were persecuted, and eventually forced to leave the south of France and take refuge in certain valleys of Piedmont subject to the Duke of Savoy. Susa, to the south-east of Mont Cenis, became (and remains) their chief centre. Thenceforth they were commonly called Vaudois, after the Canton Vaud.

In January 1655 the Duke of Savoy issued an edict that the Vaudois must, within a few days, either join the Church of Rome or quit his territory—under pain of death if they resisted. Their remonstrances were in vain, and in April an army was sent to enforce the edict.

A general massacre took place among those who had refused to leave, or to profess the Roman Catholic faith; some escaped, however, into the mountains and appealed to England for help. The news of the event aroused great sympathy in this country, and Cromwell ordered a national fast and subscription (which amounted to £40,000) for the benefit of the survivors; he also sent an envoy bearing a letter of remonstrance to the Duke, and urged the Protestant powers of Europe to make similar intercession. His efforts proved successful, the survivors being permitted to return to their homes and retain their forms of worship. As Latin Secretary to the Committee of Foreign Affairs (see p. xvii), Milton composed all the despatches sent by Cromwell in connection with the event. They are printed among his "Letters of State." This Sonnet, of course, is far stronger in expression of feeling.

The following extract is from the despatch to Charles X. of Sweden and is typical of the Letters: "We make no question but that the fame of that most rigid edict has reached your dominions, whereby the duke of Savoy has totally ruined his protestant subjects inhabiting the Alpine valleys...so that many being killed, the rest stripped and exposed to most certain destruction are now forced to wander over desert mountains, and through perpetual winter, together with their wives and children, half dead with cold and hunger... Therefore we make it our chief request that you would solicit the duke of Savoy by letters, and, by interposing your intermediating authority, endeavour to avert the horrid cruelty of this edict"—*P. W.* II. 252, 253.

3. *who kept thy truth.* Cf. Milton's tract *The Likeliest Means to Remove Hirelings out of the Church*, 1659: "those ancientest reformed churches of the Waldenses—if they rather continued not pure since the apostles"; and again, "the Waldenses, our first reformers" (*P. W.* III. pp. 16, 32). So in the "Letters of State" he speaks of them as

"ancient professors of the orthodox faith," and "for many years remarkably famous for embracing the *purity* of religion"—*P. W.* II. 254, 259.

At that time the sect of Vaudois was supposed to be of great antiquity, reaching back almost to the Apostolic era. But, as stated above, their origin cannot historically be placed earlier than the end of the 12th century. Their worship was of a most simple character.

4. A reference, characteristic of Milton, to the pre-Reformation times in England, and to what he considered idolatrous practices in worship. (See *Christian Doctrine* II. v.)

5. *in thy Book.* See *Revelation* xx. 12.

7, 8. Sir Samuel Morland, Cromwell's envoy to the Duke of Savoy, published in 1658 a history of the Vaudois and an account of the massacre. He relates (and gives an illustration of) an incident such as these lines describe: "A mother was hurled down a mighty rock, with a little infant in her arms; and three days after was found dead with the little child alive, but fast clasped between the arms of the dead mother which were cold and stiffe, insomuch that those who found them had much ado to get the young childe out." Morland's history of the sect was taken mainly from MSS. with which leading members of the Vaudois had furnished him at Turin. He afterwards gave them to the University of Cambridge (having himself been at Magdalene College), and they are now in the University Library. Unfortunately they were for the most part forgeries, designed to prove the tradition of the antiquity of the sect. See the *National Dictionary of Biography.*

In England many prints of these scenes of massacre were published, and "operated like Fox's 'Book of Martyrs'" in exciting horror of the Church of Rome.—*Warton.*

9. *redoubled,* re-echoed.

10. He is thinking of Tertullian's famous saying, "The blood of martyrs is the seed of the church."

11. *the Italian fields.* Cf. *P. L.* I. 520, "Fled over Adria to the Hesperian fields," i.e. Italy; and *Comus,* 60, "Roving the Celtic and Iberian fields," i.e. France and Spain.

12, 13. *The triple tyrant,* the Pope; an allusion to the Papal tiara surrounded with three crowns. *who,* those who.

14. The Puritans interpreted the Babylon, "that great city," of the Book of *Revelation* to be the Church of Rome. By "Babylonian woe" Milton means, I suppose, the destruction foretold in *Rev.* xviii.; but some interpret it "Antichrist."

NOTES. 55

XIX.

Milton "speaks with great modesty of himself, as if he had not five, or two, but only one talent."—*Newton*.

2. *Ere half my days*; not to be taken quite literally; he was in his 44th year when total blindness came upon him; see *Life*, p. xviii.

dark, i.e. to him in his affliction. Cf. *P. L.* VII. 27, and *Samson Agonistes*, 80, 81, where the poet is thinking of his own state.

wide; the epithet is beautifully suggestive of a blind man's feeling of helplessness, and the effect is increased by the alliteration.

3. An allusion to the parable of the talents, *Matthew* xxv. 14—30. *that one talent*; his poetic faculty; see Sonnet II., last note.

7. He seems to have *John* ix. 4 in mind. No "*day*-labour" can be expected of him because he only knows an unbroken "night, when no man can work."

8. *fondly*, foolishly; see G. *prevent*, check, forestall (*prævenire*).

12. *thousands*, i.e. of angelic beings. In *Christian Doctrine*, I. IX. Milton discusses "The Special Government of Angels" in relation to this world, and their execution of the commands of the Almighty. Among texts which he quotes are *Zechariah* i. 10, iv. 10, *Rev.* v. 6.

13. *post*, speed, hasten; a common Shakespearian word; cf. *Julius Cæsar*, III. 1. 287, "Post back with speed, and tell him what hath chanced."

14. *They also*, those other angels too—in contrast to the "thousands" just mentioned.

stand; cf. *Luke* i. 19, "I am Gabriel, that stand in the presence of God"; and *Daniel* vii. 10.

This Sonnet is illustrated by *Appendix*, I. and v., pp. 67, 68, 75, 76.

XX.

Written probably about 1656.

The friend addressed was a son of the Puritan statesman and writer Henry Lawrence (1600—1664), a kinsman of Cromwell and "Lord President of the Council" of State for several years (1653—1659). As secretary, Milton must have been brought into contact with Henry Lawrence—perhaps knew him at Cambridge, where he was a member of the Puritan College Emmanuel, 1622—1627. There is a eulogistic allusion to him in the *Second Defence* (*P. W.* I. 293). Phillips in his

Life specially mentions one of Lawrence's sons—no doubt, the one addressed in these lines—as a frequent visitor at Milton's house. If it was the eldest son, the Sonnet gains a pathetic interest from the fact that he died so soon after (in 1657).

"The two sonnets [XX, XXI] are the best, perhaps the only successful, experiments in the lighter style, which Milton has made... The cast of these sonnets as notes of invitation is suggested by Horace, II. *Carm.* II, I, 'Quid bellicosus Cantaber' &c."—*Mark Pattison.*

1. An imitation of Horace's line *O matre pulchra filia pulchrior*—*Odes* I. 16. 1.

4, 5. *waste*, spend; see G. *what;* the object of *gaining.* 'Making the best of the dull, cold season.'

6. *Favonius*, the south-west wind; the proverbial harbinger of spring. *reinspire*, breathe upon once more.

7. *in fresh attire;* cf. "the well-attired woodbine," *Lycidas*, 146.

8. *Matthew* vi. 28. The metaphor introduced in *clothe...attire.*

9, 10. Milton's biographers speak of him as very temperate in diet and abstemious. His feelings on the point are expressed in the sixth of his Latin *Elegies* (55—78).

10. *Attic*, simple yet refined; commonly applied to literary style, as in the phrase "Attic wit" (or "salt"=Lat. *Atticum sal*), 'refined, delicate wit.' See G.

11, 12. On Milton's love of music see pp. x, xiii, 71, 72, and the *Notes* on the Sonnet to Lawes. Describing the poet's daily habits in his latter years Johnson says that, after studying till twelve o'clock, he "then took some exercise for an hour; then dined, then played on the organ, and sang, or heard another sing," and then studied again till six (*Life* of Milton).

Next to the organ, the lute seems to have been his favourite instrument; they are the two instruments specially mentioned in the section on music in his treatise *On Education* (*P. IV.* III. 476).

A friend whose playing on the lute had often given him much pleasure was Henry Lawes; see p. 44.

12. Cf. *L'Allegro*, 135—150. *Tuscan;* in the general sense 'Italian.' Cf. Tennyson, *In Memoriam*, LXXXIX., "the Tuscan poets." On his foreign tour (1638, 1639) Milton purchased a quantity of Italian music and shipped it home from Venice.

13, 14. 'He who can appreciate such pleasures and yet refrain from treating himself to them often, is wise: they should be enjoyed sparingly.' *oft*; emphatic; contrast "sometimes" in 3.

NOTES.   57

13. *spare to*, abstain from; cf. the use in Latin of an infinitive after *parcere*. Some interpret (wrongly?) 'spare the time to interpose.'

14. *interpose*; suggests the idea of interrupting serious pursuits.

not unwise; an example of *meiosis*, a figure of speech which Milton uses often in *P. L.*; cf. III. 32. So in Sonnet XXI. "no mean"= great (line 2).

XXI.

Written perhaps about 1657; similar in sentiment (5, 6, 11—14) and familiar style to Sonnet XX.

Cyriac Skinner, a lawyer and member of Harrington's political club called "the Rota," had been one of Milton's pupils. He was a special favourite of the poet, lived near him for some years, and was among the frequent visitors who read to him and acted as occasional amanuenses.

1. *grandsire;* Sir Edward Coke, 1552—1634; the celebrated judge and law-writer. His second daughter married William Skinner, father of Cyriac.

2. *Themis;* the goddess of law and justice.

3. *in his volumes.* Coke's chief legal works were the *Reports* and *Institutes of the Laws of England*.

4. *bar*, i.e. of the courts of law; cf. 'barrister.' *wrench*, twist, distort; see G.

5. *drench*, steep; akin to *drown*, which is more commonly used in this metaphorical way; cf. *The Passionate Pilgrim*, 113, "And I in deep delight am chiefly drowned."

6. *after*, afterwards.

7, 8. i.e. dismiss from your thoughts both mathematical and scientific studies, and foreign politics.

Mr Mark Pattison reminds us that about the middle of the 17th century there was a great development in England of the study of science and natural philosophy: a movement marked by the foundation of the Royal Society in 1660. See Evelyn's *Diary* often; and Pepys.

8. Milton was thinking of Horace's stanza (*Odes*, II. II. 1—4):

> *Quid bellicosus Cantaber et Scythes,*
> *Hirpine Quinti, cogitet Hadria*
>   *Divisus objecto, remittas*
>   *Quaerere.*

what the Swede intends; dependent on *let rest*='do not trouble about.'

intends; so the Cambridge MS.; the 1673 edition has *intend*.

Charles X. of Sweden was then at war with Poland and Russia. Among the 'Letters of State' written by Milton at this period there are several to Charles.

A treaty between England and France was made in 1655 and a defensive alliance in 1657. In the Netherlands the armies of Louis XIV. were vanquishing the Spanish. Altogether, France and French politics must have been a good deal in people's thoughts.

9. *betimes*, early, in good time. Originally *by time*.

11. 'We are not to be always occupied with serious matters.'

XXII.

The time reference in the first line indicates that the Sonnet was written in 1655, the date of Milton's complete loss of sight being 1652. The poem was first printed by Phillips in 1694; the tone of lines 9—15 prevented its being published in the 1673 edition.

1, 2. Similarly in the *Second Defence* he says of his eyes, "so little do they betray any external appearance of injury, that they are as unclouded and bright as the eyes of those who see most distinctly" (*P. W.* I. 235).

Probably the disease from which he suffered was amaurosis or disease of the optic nerve, since that commonly makes no external change in the eye. Cf. the passage on his blindness in *P. L.* III. 22—26:

"thou (Light)
Revisit'st not these eyes, that roll in vain
To find thy piercing ray, and find no dawn;
So thick a *drop serene* hath quenched their *orbs*,
Or dim suffusion veiled."

The expression "drop serene" is a literal rendering of *gutta serena*, the technical Latin term for "complete amaurosis," i.e. amaurosis in its worst form. On Milton's blindness, see also pp. 75, 76.

1. *this three years' day;* cf. 2 *Henry VI.* II. 1. 2, "I saw not better sport these seven years' day."

4. *orbs*, eye-balls; cf. *oculorum orbes* in *Æneid*, XII. 670; and ὀμμάτων κύκλοι, e.g. in the *Antigone*, 974.

7. *bate*, abate; an 'aphetised,' i.e. shortened, form.

8. *bear up;* a nautical metaphor; 'to sail, take one's course, towards.' Cf. *Othello*, I. 3. 8, "A Turkish fleet, and bearing up to Cyprus"; so in *The Tempest*, III. 2. 3, "bear up and board' em."

10. *conscience*, consciousness; see G.

NOTES.

11. *In liberty's defence,* i.e. by writing his first *Defence of the English People* (*Pro populo Anglicano defensio*), 1651. See *Life,* p. xviii.

In the exordium (*P. W.* I. 216—222) of the *Second Defence,* 1654, Milton speaks in most exalted terms of the services which he supposed himself to have rendered by the first *Defence* to the cause of liberty, and of the impression which he had created abroad. His words, he thinks, were addressed not merely to his own countrymen but to "the whole collective body of people, cities, states, and councils of the wise and eminent, through the wide expanse of anxious and listening Europe" (p. 219).

12. *talks;* so the Cambridge MS.; changed by Phillips to *rings,* merely in imitation, I suppose, of the first line of Sonnet XV (also one of the Sonnets first published in Phillips's *Life*). Almost all editors adopt *rings* as a more poetical word than *talks;* yet in the numerous other instances in which the text of the four Sonnets first printed by Phillips differs from the Cambridge MS., the latter, which gives us the poems as written or dictated by Milton, is now universally followed. To depart from this principle in a single case (which moreover is so readily explained by the theory of imitation) seems to me very arbitrary.

13. *mask;* we use 'masquerade' in this metaphorical sense.

XXIII.

Perhaps Raleigh's Sonnet "*A Vision upon The Faerie Queene*" suggested to M. "the idea of a Sonnet in the form of a Vision."

Milton's first wife died in 1652. In November 1656 he married Catherine Woodcock, who died fifteen months later (February, 1658) in childbirth. Of her we know nothing more than this Sonnet tells us. Probably it was written in 1658. Its pathos is heightened by the fact that Milton had never *seen* his wife.

1—4. The story how Alcestis, wife of Admetus, king of Pheræ in Thessaly, died in place of her husband but was brought back from the lower world by Hercules ("Jove's great son"), is told in the *Alcestis* of Milton's favourite Euripides; cf. Browning, *Balaustion's Adventure.*

3. Admetus, thanking Hercules, addresses him, ὦ τοῦ μεγίστου Ζηνὸς εὐγενὲς τέκνον—*Alcestis,* 1136.

5, 6. Alluding to the ceremonies for purification after childbirth enjoined by the Mosaic Law—*Leviticus* xii. *as whom,* as one whom.

10. *Her face was veiled;* as was the face of Alcestis at first when Hercules brought her back into her husband's presence.

14. Cf. *P. L.* VIII. 478—480. *night,* i.e. of blindness.

SONNETS.

ON THE NEW FORCERS OF CONSCIENCE UNDER THE LONG PARLIAMENT.

In the 1673 edition (where it is first printed) this poem is not placed among the Sonnets. Strictly, it belongs to the *genus* Sonnet; written in Italian, it would certainly be treated as a Sonnet, for the type (*Sonetto Codato*, "Tailed Sonnet") was recognised by Italian poets and critics. But the poem is irregular according to the normal principles of the structure of the English Sonnet, and among Milton's editors there has always been difference of opinion how to class it. Some place it—unnumbered—at the end of the Sonnets, and this seems to me the best plan. It must however be read in close connection with Sonnets XI, XII, since their under-current of hostility to Presbyterianism here finds full vent: Milton speaks as an Independent, and pleads for liberty of conscience. Date of composition about 1646–47.

Regarding the piece as a Sonnet "strictly conformed to the Italian model," Mr Mark Pattison says: "It is of the form called 'colla coda,' a form which seems to have been introduced as early as the fifteenth century, and was much used by a Rabelaisian Florentine satirist who went by the name of Burchiello. From him was derived the denomination Burchielleschi, applied to a species of homely and familiar verse. This form went out of fashion during the sixteenth century, but was revived at the beginning of the seventeenth, and Milton may have met with sonnets of this burlesque form in circulation at Florence. At any rate, in this sonnet alone we have sufficient evidence that Milton went to Italian models for his sonnets." No doubt, Milton selected this class of composition because of its traditional use for colloquial satire. The phrase "forcers of conscience" occurs in *Of Civil Power* (II. 532).

1. The resolution of the Commons to abolish Episcopacy, adopted in September 1642, was formally passed in October 1646. The words "thrown off your Prelate Lord" may have special reference to this formal abolition of Prelacy, or merely allude in general terms to the efforts of the Commons to crush the Episcopal system of the Church and substitute Presbyterianism.

2. *renounced his Liturgy*. The public and even private use of the *Book of Common Prayer* was forbidden by the Commons in 1645.

3. "The parochial endowments were not confiscated, and as many of the clergy left their livings rather than conform to the Presbyterian

government and ritual, there was much preferment vacant, and consequently much scramble for it"—*Mark Pattison*. Moreover under the new system there was just as much pluralism as under the old, i.e. holding of more than one post (for the sake of salary) by the same minister.

5. *for this*, for this purpose, i.e. to be pluralists. *adjure the civil sword*, i.e. call in the power of the State to enforce submission to Presbyterianism. This the Presbyterians were very ready to do. In fact, Milton found that as regards toleration and liberty of opinion in religious questions nothing had been gained by the overthrow of the Laudian system; cf. line 20, note.

6, 7. *consciences...free;* cf. Sonnet XVI. 13. *ride*, override, oppress.

classic hierarchy. Under the Presbyterian organization the *classis* is the synod or council composed of all the ministers and lay-elders of a town or district. It has certain powers over the ministry and religious affairs of the district which it represents. When Presbyterianism was established in England, the country was divided into provinces instead of dioceses, and each province was subdivided according to *classes*. The province, i.e. diocese, of London had twelve of these *classes* or synods.

In his pamphlet *Observations on the Articles* (1649) of the peace made with Ireland Milton attacks the Presbytery of Belfast, and speaking of the civil powers it claimed, says, "we are sure that pulpits and church-assemblies, whether *classical* or provincial, never were intended or allowed by wise magistrates to advance such purposes"— *P. W.* II. 190. He sneers at their "*classic* priestship," and their "parochial, *classical*, and provincial *hierarchies*" (pp. 192, 194).

8. *A. S.*, Adam Steuart, a Scotsman resident in London, who published several pamphlets upholding strict Presbyterianism against the views of the Independents who advocated toleration. His works appeared under the initials "A. S."; hence the contemptuous curtness of the allusion to him here.

Samuel Rutherford was one of the four Scots ministers who sat in the Westminster Assembly of Divines and drew up a Presbyterian system for England. He too belonged to the strict set of Presbyterians, and opposed the Independents. He was for some time professor at St Andrew's and a prolific writer of theological pamphlets and tracts.

12. Thomas Edwards, in a work entitled *Gangræna: or a Catalogue of many of the Errors, Heresies, Blasphemies, and pernicious Practices of the Sectaries of this Time* (1645—6) censured Milton for the opinions

expressed in his pamphlets on divorce. Edwards was a clergyman of extreme Protestant views. As one of the University preachers at Cambridge he earned the title "young Luther." Afterwards he supported Presbyterianism strongly and attacked the Independents. His allusion to Milton occurs on p. 29, part I., of the *Gangræna*—a book which created immense sensation at the time.

What-d'ye-call; a contemptuous description like "mere *A. S.*" in line 8. Dr Masson takes the reference to be to the Rev. Robert Baillie, professor at Glasgow University, and, like Rutherford, one of the Scottish members of the Westminster Assembly. In his *Dissuasive from the Errors of the Time* (1645), a pamphlet directed specially against the Independents, he condemned Milton's views of divorce in much the same style as Edwards in his *Gangræna*. Warton thought that Alexander Henderson (who died August 1646) might be meant, or George Gillespie. They were the two other members who represented Scottish Presbyterianism at Westminster. In any case the line, like Sonnet XI, shows Milton's jealous dislike of these Presbyterians from the north.

14. He means that much intriguing went on in the Westminster Assembly of Divines, and that the Assembly was unfairly constituted ("packed"), the Presbyterians being in an overwhelming majority, to the practical exclusion of the Independents (who had only five representatives) and other parties. *packing;* cf. the phrase 'to *pack* a jury.'

Trent, i.e. the Council of Trent (1545—1563), at which the representatives of the Roman Catholic Church greatly outnumbered its opponents.

15. "More than once the Parliament had rebuked the over-officiousness of the Westminster Assembly, and reminded it that it was not an authority in the realm....Especially in April 1646 there had been a case of this kind, when the Commons voted certain proceedings of the Assembly to be a breach of privilege, and intimated to the Divines that a repetition of such proceedings might subject them individually to heavy punishment"—*Masson.* Milton evidently hoped that the Commons would at last assert themselves and read the Assembly a sharp lesson.

17. *Clip your phylacteries,* curtail your hypocritical pretensions and insolence. *phylacteries;* see G. *baulk,* spare, not touch; see G.

In its original form the line ran, "Crop ye as close as marginal P—'s eares": an allusion "to the celebrated William Prynne, the Lincoln's Inn Lawyer, who had been twice pilloried and had his nose slit and his ears cut off for anti-Prelatic pamphlets by sentence of the Star-Chamber. ... Since his release from prison at the opening of the Long Parliament in 1640, Prynne had been a conspicuous Presbyterian, enforcing his views in tract after tract of a dry and learned kind, always with references to his authorities running down the margins of the pages. Prynne's want of ears and the laboured margins of his pamphlets were subjects of popular jest; but Milton had a special grudge against him on account of a reference to himself in one of the 'marginal' oddities. It was clearly in good taste, however, to erase the allusion in the Sonnet, referring as it did to a cruelty unjustly endured, under a tyrannical Government, by a brave, though thick-headed, man"—*Masson*.

Newton notes that Milton has the same allusion in his treatise on *The Likeliest Means to Remove Hirelings out of the Church*, where he speaks of Prynne as that "hot querist for tithes, whom ye may know, by his wits lying ever beside him *in the margin*, to be ever beside his wits in the text, a fierce reformer once, now rankled with a contrary heat" (*P. W.* III. 17). Similarly in *The Reason of Church Government* Milton ridicules the practice of loading the margins of controversial pamphlets with references, though he is there alluding not to Prynne but to the supporters of episcopacy, "men whose learning and belief lies in *marginal* stuffings" (*P. W.* II. 481).

19. *in your charge*, in the indictment which will be brought against you.

20. *Priest* is a contraction of *presbyter* from Gk. πρεσβύτερος 'elder,' and Milton says that they would be found to be identical not in etymology alone; i.e. that the change from 'priest' to 'presbyter' would prove no gain at all, the one being as intolerant and grasping as the other had been (according, that is, to Milton, the bitter enemy of the Church).

writ large, i.e. in full (*presbyter*), not in the abbreviated form (*priest*).

"In railing at Establishments, Milton condemned not episcopacy alone: he thought even the simple institutions of the new Reformation too rigid and arbitrary for the natural freedom of conscience: he contended for that sort of individual or personal religion, by which every man is to be his own priest. When these verses were written, Presbyterianism was triumphant; and the Independents and the Churchmen joined in one common complaint against a want of toleration"—*Warton*. See *Appendix*, IV., V., pp. 72—74.

GLOSSARY.

asp, XI. 13. Gk. ἀσπίς, Lat. *aspis*. "A very venomous serpent of Egypt, celebrated in connection with the story of Cleopatra's suicide. ...This serpent is of frequent occurrence along the Nile, and is the sacred serpent of ancient Egypt"—*Century Dict*. There is a variant form *aspick*, used in North's *Plutarch* in the account of Cleopatra's death, whence it passed into Shakespeare's *Antony and Cleopatra*, V. 2. 296, 354, and so into Tennyson's *Dream of Fair Women*, 160 ("Showing the aspick's bite").

Attic, XX. 10; lit. "of or pertaining to Attica, or to its capital, Athens; Athenian": hence "having characteristics peculiarly Athenian," i.e. of literary style, taste, etc. = "marked by simple, refined elegance."

baulk; originally (1) 'to miss, omit,' especially a place, i.e. to pass by without visiting it; hence (2) the general sense 'to pass over, ignore, refrain from touching'; and so (3) 'to neglect, not trouble about.' Cf. Shakespeare, *Lucrece*, 696, 697:
"Make slow pursuit, or altogether balk
 The prey";
where the reference is to lazy, over-fed hounds which do not trouble to hunt their game.

charm, VIII. 5. In Elizabethan writers *charm* from Lat. *carmen* usually had the strong sense 'spell, incantation'; cf. *enchant* from Lat. *incantare*. See *Samson Agonistes*, 934, "Thy fair *enchanted* cup, and warbling *charms*." Both words weakened into the notion 'pleasant, delightful,' as the belief in magic declined. In *Othello*, III. 4. 57 *charmer* = 'sorceress.'

clime, VIII. 8, 'region, land'; cf. I. 242, "Is this the region, this... the clime?" So in *2 Henry VI.* III. 2. 84, "back again unto my native clime"; and in *The Merchant of Venice*, II. 1. 10. Gk. κλίμα, 'slope,' from κλίνειν, 'to slope.' *Clime* and *climate* are 'doublets,' and 'region' was the original sense of each; then, because the temperature of a region is its most important quality, both words came to mean 'temperature.'

conscience, XXII. 10, 'consciousness'; cf. *P. L.* VIII. 502, "Her virtue and the conscience of her worth." So in *Hebrews* x. 2, "because that the worshippers once purged should have had no more conscience of sins"; and 1 *Corinthians* viii. 7.

fee, XII. 7; much used as a legal term in connection with the possession or tenure of land. Thus *fee-simple* = hereditary land, held without any conditions and 'for ever.' See Shakespeare, who is fond of legal terms—*Hamlet*, II. 2. 73, IV. 4. 22; *Troilus and Cressida*,

III. 2. 53, V. 1. 26. A. S. *feoh* (cf. Germ. *vieh*) meant (1) 'cattle,' (2) 'property'—cattle being the chief kind of property in a primitive state of society. Cf. Lat. *pecunia* from *pecus*.

fondly, XIX. 8, 'foolishly'; cf. *Lycidas*, 56, "Ay me! I fondly dream." Originally *fond* was the past participle of a Middle English verb *fonnen*, 'to act like a fool,' from *fon*, 'a fool.' This sense 'foolish' is common in Elizabethan writers; cf. *Lear*, IV. 7. 60, "I am a very foolish fond old man." So in the *Prayer-Book*, "a fond thing vainly invented" ('Articles of Religion,' XXII.). The root is Scandinavian.

imp, XV. 8; a falconer's term for "inserting a feather into the wing of a hawk, or other bird, in place of one that is broken." Cf. *Richard II.* II. 1. 292, "*Imp* out our drooping country's *broken wing*"; and Massinger's *Renegado* (1624), V. 8:

"strive to *imp*
New feathers to the *broken wings* of time."

Milton, unlike Shakespeare, seldom uses sporting-terms. Middle English *impen* = 'to graft'; an *imp* is literally 'a graft, offspring.'

jolly, I. 4, 'pleasant, genial'; here it suggests the joyousness of spring-tide. In Elizabethan English *jolly* (F. *joli*) often meant 'gay, festive' in a good sense; its present (vulgar) use illustrates the general tendency of words to deteriorate in sense. F. *joli* is really of Scandinavian origin, from the root 'to revel' which we have in *Yule* = Christmas, the time of rejoicing.

phylacteries; from Gk. φυλακτήριον, 'a safeguard—amulet.' They were pieces of parchment inscribed with passages from the Law of Moses which the Jews were bidden to wear as "frontlets" on the forehead and left arm (*Exodus* xiii. 1—16, *Deuteronomy* vi. 4—8, xi. 13—18). From *Matthew* xxiii. 5 we associate them more particularly with "the scribes and Pharisees"; and "to wear broad phylacteries" has become a proverbial synonym of hypocrisy.

purple, XIV. 10; much used by poets to denote any rich colour, i.e. not limited to what is strictly called 'purple'; cf. the similar wide use of Gk. πορφύρεος and Lat. *purpureus*. Here perhaps *purple* means no more than 'lustrous, radiant'; or, if any particular colour be intended, 'rosy'—cf. *P. L.* VII. 29, 30 where the dawn is said to "purple the east" = tinge with rosy hues.

quire, XIII. 10; the older form of *choir*; each from Lat. *chorus*. Cf. the *Prayer-Book*, "In quires and places where they sing." *Quire* was one of the Latin words introduced through Christianity into A. S. We sometimes find *quirister* = chorister.

ruth, IX. 8, 'pity'; once elsewhere in Milton—cf. *Lycidas*, 163, "Look homeward, Angel, now, and melt with ruth." Shakespeare, *Troilus and Cressida*, V. 3. 48, has, "Spur them to ruthful work, rein them from ruth," where *ruthful*='piteous'; contrast *ruthless*. Akin to A. S. *hreówan*, 'to rue,' Germ. *reue*, 'repentance.'

saints, XVIII. 1; a favourite word with Milton and with the Puritans, in the general sense 'righteous men,' 'true Christians': many members of the party of Republican Independents called themselves 'saints.' Cf. *P. L.* III. 330, IV. 762. The use is Scriptural; cf. the Epistles of St Paul often, e.g. *Romans* xvi. 2, 15.

sonnet; F. *sonnet*, from Ital. *sonetto*, a diminutive of *sono*, 'sound, tune' (cf. Lat. *sonus*). The Sonnet was introduced into English literature a little before the middle of the 16th century. At first the word was not limited to the particular kind of poem now called a 'sonnet.' Thus "the very true sonnet" mentioned in *Twelfth Night*, III. 4. 25 was a ballad.

spray, I. 1; now='sprig,' especially one plucked from a tree or flower; but in Elizabethan writers it seems to have had the wider sense 'branch'; cf. *Richard II.* III. 4. 34, "Cut off the heads of too fast growing sprays." See also 2 *Henry VI.* II. 3. 45; and *P. R.* IV. 437.

virtue, X. 5, 'courage, valour'—the predominant sense of Lat. *virtus*, from *vir*, 'a man.' Cf. the *Life* of Coriolanus in North's *Plutarch* (the source of Shakespeare's Roman plays): "In those days, valiantness was honoured in Rome above all other virtues: which they call *virtus*, by the name of virtue itself, as including in that general name all other special virtues besides. So that *virtus* in the Latin was as much as valiantness" (Skeat's ed., p. 2). So in *Coriolanus*, II. 2. 87, 88.

waste, XX. 4, 'spend'; a Shakespearian use. Cf. *Midsummer-Night's Dream*, II. 1. 57, "A merrier hour was never wasted there"; and *The Tempest*, V. 301—303:

"My poor cell, where you shall take your rest
For this one night; which, part of it, I'll waste
With such discourse" etc.

wrench, XXI. 4. Used similarly, with a legal colouring, in 2 *Henry IV.* II. 1. 120, where the Chief Justice says to Falstaff: "I am well acquainted with your manner of wrenching the true cause the false way." The literal idea is 'to twist, sprain'; hence the figurative notion of 'crookedness, perversion,' which the noun *wrenche* always has in Middle English.

APPENDIX.

This **Appendix** *is meant to supplement the* **Notes** *by quoting some of the illustrative passages which they merely refer to. Most of the passages are from Milton's prose works, which to many students are not, I suppose, easily accessible.*

I.

MILTON'S GREAT PURPOSE.

SONNETS II., XIX.

THESE Sonnets illustrate the signal feature of Milton's life, viz. his purpose of writing a great poem. Sonnet II. was inserted in a letter to one of his friends. The letter[1] is a valuable comment on both Sonnets, but especially the earlier (1631). He says:

"SIR, Besides that in sundry other respects I must acknowledge me to profit by you whenever we meet, you are often to me, and were yesterday especially, as a good watchman to admonish that the hours of the night pass on (for so I call my life as yet obscure and unserviceable to mankind) and that the day with me is at hand, wherein Christ commands all to labor while there is light[2]: which because I am persuaded you do to no other purpose, than out of a true desire that God should be honor'd in everyone, I therefore think myself bound, though unask'd, to give you account, as oft as occasion is, of this my tardy moving, according to the precept of my conscience, which I firmly trust is not without God." His "tardy moving," he proceeds,

---

[1] Transcribed in Newton's edition, whence it is here copied, from the Cambridge MSS.
[2] John ix. 4. See Sonnet XIX. 7.

is not due to any taste for "affected solitariness" or that pedantic love of learning whereby the recluse "cuts himselfe off from all action." Rather, his present inaction springs from a deep sense of responsibility, from the feeling that he must prepare himself to the very best of his ability for his great work, and thus be "more fit," though "late," when he does set about it.

"The love of learning, as it is the pursuit of something good, it would sooner follow the more excellent and supreme good known and presented, and so be quickly diverted from the empty and fantastic chase of shadows and notions to the solid good flowing from due and timely obedience to that command[1] in the Gospel set out by the terrible seizing[2] of him that hid the talent. It is more probable therefore that not the endless delight of speculation, but this very consideration of that great commandment, does not press forward, as soon as many do, to undergo, but keeps off with a sacred reverence and religious advisement how best to undergo; not taking thought of being late, so it give advantage to be more fit; for those that were latest lost nothing, when the master of the vineyard came to give each one his hire[3]."

The period of self-preparation indicated by this letter accompanying the second Sonnet (1631) extends unbroken up to his Italian journey (1638). On Sept. 7, 1637, he writes to a friend to make excuse for his remissness as a correspondent: "It is my way to suffer no impediment, no love of ease, no avocation whatever, to chill the ardour, to break the continuity, or divert the completion of my literary pursuits. From this and no other reasons it often happens that I do not readily employ my pen in any gratuitous exertions[4]."

In the same month, on the 23rd, he tells the same friend, who had made enquiry as to his occupations and plans: "I am sure that you wish me to gratify your curiosity, and to let you know what I have been doing, or am meditating to do. Hear me, my Diodati, and suffer me for a moment to speak, without blushing, in a more lofty strain. Do you ask what I am meditating? By the help of Heaven, an immortality of fame. But what am I doing? πτεροφυῶ, I am letting my wings grow and preparing to fly; but my Pegasus has not yet

---

[1] i.e. the command implied in the Parable of the Talents, viz. that man should make a full use of his talents and of all that is committed to him.
[2] *Matthew* xxv. 30.
[3] *Matthew* xx.
[4] *P. W.* III. 492.

feathers enough to soar aloft in the fields of air[1]." Four years later we find a similar admission—"I have not yet completed to my mind the full circle of my private studies[2]."

This last sentence was written in 1640 (or 1641). Meanwhile his resolution had been confirmed by the friendly and flattering encouragement of Italian men of letters.

"In[3] the private academies[4] of Italy, whither I was favoured to resort, perceiving that some trifles[5] which I had in memory, composed at under twenty or thereabout, (for the manner is, that every one must give some proof of his wit and reading there,) met with acceptance above what was looked for; and other things[6], which I had shifted in scarcity of books and conveniences to patch up amongst them, were received with written encomiums, which the Italian is not forward to bestow on men of this side of the Alps; I began thus far to assent both to them and divers of my friends here at home, and not less to an inward prompting which now grew daily upon me, that by labour and intense study (which I take to be my portion in this life), joined with the strong propensity of nature, I might perhaps leave something so written to aftertimes, as they should not willingly let it die."

This "inward prompting," thus openly announced in the *Reason of Church Government* (1641), but privately indicated, as we have seen, ten years earlier, was still unsatisfied when he wrote Sonnet XIX., which should be read side by side with Sonnet II.

II.

REFERENCES TO EURIPIDES AND PINDAR.

SONNETS VIII., XXIII.

Euripides is said to have been one of Milton's favourite authors. In *The Reason of Church Government* (1641) he speaks of "those dramatic constitutions wherein Sophocles and Euripides reign" (i.e. are supreme). In the tract *On Education* (1644) he mentions the

---

[1] *P. W.* III. 495.
[2] *Church Government, P. W.* II. 476.
[3] *Church Government, P. W.* II. 477, 478.
[4] He refers to literary societies or clubs, of which there were several at Florence, e.g. the Della Crusca, the Svogliati, etc.
[5] i.e. Latin pieces; the *Elegies*, as well as some of the poems included in his *Sylvæ*, were written before he was twenty-one.
[6] Among the Latin poems which date from his Italian journey are the lines *Ad Salsillum*, a few of the *Epigrams*, and *Mansus*.

Alcestis (cf. Sonnet XXIII.) as one of the classical plays particularly suitable to be read by young students. In the Preface to *Samson Agonistes* (1671) he says that the style of a tragedy and development of plot can be properly understood only by those "who are not unacquainted with Æschylus, Sophocles, and Euripides, the three tragic poets unequalled yet by any, and the best rule to all who endeavour to write Tragedy." Compare too the reference to the classical dramatists in the famous passage on Athens in *Paradise Regained* (IV. 261—266):

> "'Thence what the lofty grave tragedians taught
> In chorus or iambic, teachers best
> Of moral prudence, with delight received
> In brief sententious precepts, while they treat
> Of fate and chance and change in human life,
> High actions and high passions best describing";

where editors note that the allusion to "brief sententious precepts" ($\gamma\nu\hat{\omega}\mu\alpha\iota$) specially fits Euripides. See also *Il Penseroso*, 97—102.

Milton has several interesting references to Pindar besides that in Sonnet VIII.—e.g. "those magnific odes and hymns, wherein Pindarus and Callimachus are in most things worthy" (*Church Government*); "Dorian lyric odes" (*P. R.* IV. 257). Compare also his sixth *Elegy*, 21—26:

> "Quid nisi vina, rosasque, racemiferumque Lyæum,
>   Cantavit brevibus Tëia Musa modis?
> Pindaricosque inflat numeros Teumesius Euan,
>   Et redolet sumptum pagina quæque merum;
> Dum gravis everso currus crepat axe supinus,
>   Et volat Eleo pulvere fuscus eques:"

lines which Cowper renders:

> "What in brief numbers sang Anacreon's Muse?
> Wine, and the rose that sparkling wine bedews.
> Pindar with Bacchus glows—his every line
> Breathes the rich fragrance of inspiring wine,
> While, with loud crash o'erturned, the chariot lies,
> And brown with dust the fiery courser flies."

APPENDIX. 71

III.

MILTON AND MUSIC.

Sonnets XIII., XX.

The love of music which brought Milton into contact with Henry Lawes and which we see in Sonnets XIII. and XX. is illustrated by a passage in his treatise *On Education*. Exercise, he says, in certain athletic sports should form part of the daily training of students and be followed by an interval of rest. This interval "may, both with profit and delight, be taken up in recreating and composing their travailed spirits with the solemn and divine harmonies of music, heard or learned; either whilst the skilful organist plies his grave and fancied descant in lofty fugues, or the whole symphony with artful and unimaginable touches adorn and grace the well-studied chords of some choice composer; sometimes the lute or soft organ-stop waiting on elegant voices, either to religious, martial, or civil ditties; which, if wise men[1] and prophets be not extremely out[2], have a great power over dispositions and manners, to smooth and make them gentle from rustic harshness and distempered passions (*P. W.* III. 475, 476)."

It is scarcely necessary to say that he uses musical terms, to which he is very partial, with perfect correctness: witness the instances in the above passage. For "fugue" see *P. L.* XI. 563, and for "descant" (=the variations added to a plain song or melody in its simplest form) compare *P. L.* IV. 603, where it is applied to the varied notes of the nightingale, and *S. A.* 1228. His use of "symphony" to mean 'a company of musicians playing in harmony' may seem curious, the word being now limited, as a musical term, to a particular kind of composition; but it then had the general sense 'harmony' in accordance with its derivation (Gk συμφωνία). Thus in *P. L.* I. 712 ("dulcet symphonies and voices sweet") it refers to the strains of instruments accompanying voices. "Touch"—see Sonnet XX. 11—was a favourite poetic word to indicate the action of the hand on a musical instrument. Cf. *P. L.* IV. 686, "With heavenly touch of instrumental sounds." So in *The Merchant of Venice*, V. 56, 57:

"soft stillness and the night
Become the touches of sweet harmony";

[1] Editors note that the allusion is primarily to Plato, more especially to the third book of the *Republic*.
[2] i.e. are not entirely mistaken.

and *The Passionate Pilgrim*, 107, 108:

"whose *heavenly touch*
Upon the lute doth ravish human sense."

"Ditty" was applicable to any kind of song, i.e. not depreciatory then as now. Milton evidently liked the lute much (Sonnet XX. 11, *P. L.* V. 151, *Ode on the Passion*, 28), and the frequent allusions to it in Shakespeare prove its popularity in Elizabethan times. But his favourite instrument was the organ; see the oft-cited description of organ-playing in *P. L.* XI. 560—563, and the account of the mechanism of the organ in *P. L.* I. 708, 709. Other notable passages on music in his works are *L'Allegro*, 135—150, *Il Penseroso*, 161—166, *Comus*, 244—264, *P. L.* VII. 594—599.

IV.

MILTON AND THE PRESBYTERIANS.

SONNET XVI.: "On the New Forcers of Conscience."

Milton had once been in sympathy with the Presbyterian party, but much in their action offended him no less than his views on divorce (see Sonnets XI., XII.) offended them. The bitterness against the Presbyterian ministry which animates his lines "On the New Forcers of Conscience" (1646—47) and prompted the appeal (1652) to Cromwell (Sonnet XVI.) might be illustrated by numerous passages of his prose works. The following from *The Tenure of Kings and Magistrates* (1649) is an example. After admonishing their political leaders "not to compel unforcible things, in religion especially," he continues:

"I have something also to the divines, though brief to [i.e. compared to] what were needful; not to be disturbers of the civil affairs, being in hands better able and more belonging to manage them; but to study harder, and to attend the office of good pastors... which if they ever well considered, how little leisure would they find, to be the most pragmatical sidesmen of every popular tumult and sedition! and all this while are to learn what the true end and reason is of the gospel which they teach; and what a world it differs from the censorious and supercilious *lording over conscience*[1]. It would be good

---

[1] The italics throughout are mine, and draw attention to resemblances, often of phrase as well as of substance, to "The New Forcers" and Sonnet XVI.

also they lived so as might persuade the people they hated covetousness, which, worse than heresy, is idolatry; hated *pluralities*, and all kind of simony; left rambling from benefice to benefice, *like ravenous wolves seeking where they may devour the biggest.* Of which if some, well and warmly seated from the beginning, be not guilty, it were good they held not conversation with such as are. Let them be sorry, that, being called to assemble about reforming the church, they fell to progging and soliciting the parliament, though they had *renounced the name of priests, for a new settling of their tithes and oblations.* Let them assemble in consistory with their elders and deacons, according to ancient ecclesiastical rule, to the preserving of church discipline, each in his several charge, and not a *pack* of clergymen by themselves to bellycheer in their presumptuous Sion, or to promote designs, abuse [deceive] and gull the simple laity, and stir up tumult, as the *prelates* did, for the maintenance of their pride and avarice...[For] if they be the ministers of mammon instead of Christ, and scandalize his church with the filthy love of gain, aspiring also to sit the closest and the heaviest of all *tyrants upon the conscience*, and fall notoriously into the same sins, whereof so lately and loud they accused the prelates; as God rooted out those, so will he root out them, their imitators (*P. W.* II. 36, 37)."

V.

"FREE CONSCIENCE."

SONNETS XVI., XVII.: "On the New Forcers of Conscience."

There was no subject on which Milton felt more strongly than religious liberty. Almost the last of his pamphlets on the Church was *A Treatise of Civil Power in Ecclesiastical Causes* (1659), "shewing that it is not lawful for any power on earth to compel in matters of religion." The first paragraph begins:

"Two things there be, which have ever been found working much mischief to the church of God and the advancement of truth: force on one side restraining, and hire on the other side corrupting, the teachers thereof...The former shall be at this time my argument; the latter[1] as

---

[1] The payment ("hire") of ministers is discussed in the tract that followed a few months later, viz. *The Likeliest Means to Remove Hirelings out of the Church.*

I shall find God disposing me, and opportunity inviting." These are some sentences that illustrate his "argument."

"It is the general consent of all sound protestant writers, that the scripture only can be the final judge or rule in matters of religion, and that only in the conscience of every Christian to himself."..."Seeing then that in matters of religion none can judge or determine here on earth, no, not church governors themselves, against the consciences of other believers, my inference is that in those matters they[1] neither can command nor use constraint."..."Thus then, if church governors cannot use force in religion, though but for this reason, because they cannot infallibly determine to the conscience without convincement, much less have civil magistrates authority to use force where they can much[2] less judge; unless they mean only to be the civil executioners of them[3] who have no civil power to give them such commission, no, nor yet ecclesiastical, to any force or violence in religion."..."The apostle speaks [2 Cor. x.] of that spiritual power by which Christ governs his church, how all-sufficient it is, how powerful to reach the conscience, and the inward man with whom it chiefly deals, and whom no power else can deal with. In comparison of which, how ineffectual and weak is outward force with all her boisterous tools, to the shame of those Christians, and especially those churchmen[4], who to the exercising of church-discipline, never cease calling on the civil magistrate to interpose his fleshly force."..."Let them cease then to importune and interrupt the magistrate from attending to his own charge in civil and moral things.. let him also forbear force where he hath no right to judge, for the conscience is not his province." And he sums up thus:

"As to those magistrates who think it their work to settle religion, and those ministers or others who so oft call upon them to do so, I trust, that having well considered what hath been here argued, neither they will continue in that intention, nor these in that expectation from them; when they shall find that the settlement of religion belongs only to each particular church by persuasive and spiritual means within itself, and that the defence only of the church belongs to the magistrate."

---

[1] The magistrates, civil authorities.
[2] i.e. much less than the church governors.
[3] i.e. ministers of religion.
[4] Presbyterians.

VI.

MILTON'S BLINDNESS.

Sonnets XIX., XXII.

What is said as to Milton's blindness in the brief sketch of his Life (p. xviii.) and in the notes on Sonnets XIX., XXII. may be supplemented by mention of an interesting fact, viz. that he believed that his loss of physical eyesight was compensated by increased spiritual illumination. Thus he asks in a letter " Why should I not submit with complacency to this loss of sight, which seems only withdrawn from the body without, to increase the sight of the mind within?" (*P. W.* III. 513). The belief is put very vividly in the *Second Defence*, which was written (1654) two years after his blindness was complete.

"There[1] is, as the apostle has remarked, a way to strength through weakness. Let me then be the most feeble creature alive, as long as that feebleness serves to invigorate the energies of my rational and immortal spirit; as long as in that obscurity, in which I am enveloped, the light of the divine presence more clearly shines, then, in proportion as I am weak, I shall be invincibly strong; and in proportion as I am blind, I shall see more clearly. O that I may thus be perfected by feebleness, and irradiated by obscurity! And, indeed, in my blindness, I enjoy in no inconsiderable degree the favour of the Deity, who regards me with more tenderness and compassion in proportion as I am able to behold nothing but himself;...and is wont to illuminate [my obscurity] with an interior light, more precious and more pure" (*P. W.* I. 239). Compare *P. L.* III. 51—55, where, after speaking of the outer darkness that surrounds him, he ends:

" So much the rather thou, celestial Light,
Shine inward, and the mind through all her powers
Irradiate: there plant eyes, all mist from thence
Purge and disperse, that I may see and tell
Of things invisible to mortal sight."

See also *Samson Agonistes*, 1687—1689.

[1] The passage is a translation (Fellowes's), the *Second Defence* being written in Latin so that his vindication of the English people might appeal to all Europe. To the same translator we owe the version of Milton's Letters (*Epistolæ Familiares*) in Mr St John's edition of the prose works (Bohn's " Standard Library," III. 487—522), from which our extracts are made.

One of the finest allusions in literature to Milton's blindness is in Gray's lines on him in the *Progress of Poesy:*

"Nor second He, that rode sublime
Upon the seraph-wings of Extasy,
The secrets of th' Abyss to spy.
  He pass'd the flaming bounds of Place and Time:
The living Throne, the sapphire blaze,
Where Angels tremble, while they gaze[1],
He saw; but, blasted with excess of light,
Clos'd his eyes in endless night."

---

[1] A reference to *Paradise Lost*, III. 380—382:
  Thee, Father, first they sung, Omnipotent,
  Immutable, Immortal, Infinite,
  Eternal King; thee, Author of all being,
  Fountain of light, thyself invisible
  Amidst the glorious brightness where thou sitt'st
  Throned inaccessible, but when thou shadest
  The full blaze of thy beams, and through a cloud
  Drawn round about thee like a radiant shrine
  Dark with excessive bright thy skirts appear,
  Yet dazzle Heaven, that brightest Seraphim
  Approach not, but with both wings veil their eyes.

I. GENERAL INDEX TO THE NOTES.

Alcestis, story of in Euripides, 59
Aldersgate-street, Milton's house in, 36
Babylon, "that great city," 54
Bucer, Martin, professor at Cambridge, 43
Casella, friend of Dante, 46
Chæronea, battle of, 40
Charles X. of Sweden 53, 58
Cheke, Sir John, 42; pupils at Cambridge, 43
Church and State, Milton's opinion with regard to, 50, 52
"classic hierarchy" of the Presbyterians 61
Colasterion, Milton's treatise, 42
Coke, Sir Edward, 57
Colchester, siege of, 47, 48
Colkitto, "young," 42
"Committee for the propagation of the gospel" 49
Cromwell 49, 50
Dante, Milton's love of his poetry, 46
Darwen, stream of, 50
divorce, Milton's pamphlets on, 41
Dunbar, battle of, 50
Edwards, Thomas, author of *Gangræna*, 61, 62
Electra of Euripides, story about, 37, 38
"Emathian conqueror" (Alexander) 37
"Epeirot" 51
Episcopacy 60
Euripides 38, 59
Fairfax, general, 47, 48
Favonius 56

Gillespie, George, Scotch Presbyterian, 62
Good Shepherd, parable of, 51
Gordon, Lord George, 42
Hannibal, "the African bold," 51, 52
Hours, Lat. *Horæ*, 30
"Hydra heads" 48
Isocrates, the "old man eloquent," 40
Latona, story of from Ovid, 43
Lawes, Henry, the composer, 44; music of 45
Lawrence, Henry, friend of Milton, 55, 56
Ley, James, Earl of Marlborough, 39; his daughter Lady Margaret, a friend of Milton, 39, 40
liberty 44, 59
lute, Milton's fondness for, 56
Midas, King of Phrygia, 45
Mile-End Green 41
Milton: his early resolve to write a great poem 31, 32; his appearance 32; blindness of 55, 58; abstemious habits 56; love of music 56; his second wife 59
Montrose, campaign of, 42
Morland, Sir Samuel, his history of the Vaudois, 54
nightingale and cuckoo, legend as to, 29, 31
Pindar 37
Prayer-Book, use of forbidden, 60
Presbyterians 60-63; Milton's growing dislike of 41, 50; their *classes* 61
Preston, battle of, 50

Prynne, William, 62, 63
Pyrrhus, "the fierce Epeirot," 51
Quintilian 42
Royal Society, foundation of, 57
Rutherford, Samuel, 61
Savoy, Duke of, and the Vaudois, 53
"Scotch What-d'ye-call" 62
singular verb with plural subject, 45
Skinner, Cyriac, 57
Solemn League and Covenant 48
Sonetto Codato 60
Steuart, Adam, "mere A. S.," 61
talents, parable of, 55

Tertullian, famous saying of, 54
Tetrachordon, Milton's treatise, 41, 42
Themis 57
Trent, Council of, 62
Tuscan = Italian 56
Vane, Sir Henry, "the younger," 51, 52
Vaudois or Waldenses, their sufferings, 52, 53; their religion 53, 54
Westminster Assembly of Divines 62
Worcester, battle of, 50

II. INDEX OF WORDS AND PHRASES IN THE *NOTES*.

"Attic taste" 56
bar 57
charms 37
clogs 43
"cloud of war" 50
commit 45
day-labour 55
dishonest 40
drench 57
"eye of day" 30
feastful 39
"golden rod" 47
"gowns, not arms" 51
"immortal streams" 47
interpose 57
knight-in-arms 36
maw 51
nerve 52

nightingale 30
post (verb) 55
redouble 54
shallow 30
shew'th (rhyming with *truth*) 32
"sinews of war" 52
sleek 42
spare to 57
spell 52
spleen 39
"sun's bright circle" 37
still (adj.) 30
"the triple tyrant" 54
"this three years' day" 58
"thy fill" 47
timely 30
timely-happy 32
"wreath of victory" 50

CAMBRIDGE: PRINTED BY JOHN CLAY, M.A. AT THE UNIVERSITY PRESS.

The Pitt Press Shakespeare for Schools

Edited by A. W. VERITY, M.A., with Introduction, Notes, Glossary and Index to each volume.

A MIDSUMMER-NIGHT'S DREAM.
EIGHTH EDITION. *Price* 1s. 6d.

"For schoolboys of fourteen and upwards this edition is not to be beaten, and we can congratulate Mr Verity and the University Press upon the publication of what will probably become the standard school edition of this play."—*Guardian*.

THE MERCHANT OF VENICE.
FIFTH EDITION. *Price* 1s. 6d.

"A perfect schoolboy's edition."—*School Guardian*.

KING HENRY V.
FOURTH EDITION. *Price* 1s. 6d.

"*The* school edition of the play."—*Guardian*.
"Complete, clear, and admirable in every way for use in schools."—*Bookman*.

TWELFTH NIGHT.
SEVENTH EDITION. *Price* 1s. 6d.

"It is a model of how a play of Shakespeare should be prepared so as to attract and not to repel young students."—*Athenæum*.
"This is the best school edition of the play that has come under our notice."—*Journal of Education*.

THE TEMPEST. SIXTH EDITION. *Price* 1s. 6d.

"Probably the most complete school edition that has ever been issued."—*Educational Review*.
"It would seem that the ideal school edition of Shakespeare has at last been developed."—*University Correspondent*.

The Pitt Press Shakespeare for Schools
Edited by A. W. VERITY, M.A.

KING RICHARD II.
FIFTH EDITION. *Price 1s. 6d.*

"It would be difficult to praise this work (or this series) too highly."—*School World*.

JULIUS CÆSAR. NINTH EDITION. *Price 1s. 6d.*

"We can only say that it is as good and deserves as much praise as its predecessors [*A Midsummer-Night's Dream* and *Twelfth Night*]."—*Guardian*.

KING LEAR. THIRD EDITION. *Price 1s. 6d.*

"A model edition."—*Academy*.
"Mr Verity is an ideal editor for schools."—*Bookman*.

MACBETH.
SECOND EDITION. *Price 1s. 6d.*

"Seems to us to be an excellent text-book for the study of the play."—*Education*.

AS YOU LIKE IT.
THIRD EDITION. *Price 1s. 6d.*

Student's Edition.

MACBETH. LARGER EDITION. *Price 2s. 6d.*

"An edition of rare merit, suited to the highest study of the poem."—*Guardian*.

"Mr Verity's *Macbeth* has been described as 'possibly the best' (school edition) 'that has been produced of any play of Shakespeare,' and we should not care to gainsay even so superlative an encomium."—*Practical Teacher*.

HAMLET. *Price 3s.*

"Mr Verity has made many notable contributions to Shakespearian literature, but in the 'Student's Shakespeare,' edition of *Hamlet* he has undoubtedly surpassed all previous efforts."—*Guardian*.

"The best of the kind for students that we have seen."—*National Teacher*.

CORIOLANUS. *Price 3s.*

THE PITT PRESS SERIES

AND THE

CAMBRIDGE SERIES FOR SCHOOLS AND TRAINING COLLEGES.

Volumes of the latter series are marked by a dagger †.

COMPLETE LIST.

GREEK.

Author	Work	Editor	Price
Aeschylus	Prometheus Vinctus	Rackham	2/6
Aristophanes	Aves—Plutus—Ranae	Green	3/6 *each*
,,	Vespae	Graves	3/6
,,	Acharnians	,,	3/-
,,	Nubes	,,	3/6
Demosthenes	Olynthiacs	Glover	2/6
Euripides	Heracleidae	Beck & Headlam	3/6
,,	Hercules Furens	Gray & Hutchinson	2/-
,,	Hippolytus	Hadley	2/-
,,	Iphigeneia in Aulis	Headlam	2/6
,,	Medea	,,	2/6
,,	Hecuba	Hadley	2/6
,,	Helena	Pearson	3/6
,,	Alcestis	Hadley	2/6
,,	Orestes	Wedd	4/6
Herodotus	Book IV	Shuckburgh	*In the Press*
,,	,, V	,,	3/-
,,	,, VI, VIII, IX	,,	4/- *each*
,,	,, VIII 1—90, IX 1—89	,,	2/6 *each*
Homer	Odyssey IX, X	Edwards	2/6 *each*
,,	,, XXI	,,	2/-
,,	,, XI	Nairn	2/-
,,	Iliad VI, XXII, XXIII, XXIV	Edwards	2/- *each*
,,	Iliad IX, X	Lawson	2/6
Lucian	Somnium, Charon, etc.	Heitland	3/6
,,	Menippus and Timon	Mackie	3/6
Plato	Apologia Socratis	Adam	3/6
,,	Crito	,,	2/6
,,	Euthyphro	,,	2/6
,,	Protagoras	J. & A. M. Adam	4/6

1

THE PITT PRESS SERIES, ETC.

GREEK continued.

Author	Work	Editor	Price
Plutarch	Demosthenes	Holden	4/6
,,	Gracchi	,,	6/-
,,	Nicias	,,	5/-
,,	Sulla	,,	6/-
,,	Timoleon	,,	6/-
Sophocles	Oedipus Tyrannus	Jebb	4/-
Thucydides	Book III	Spratt	5/-
,,	Book VI	,,	In the Press
,,	Book VII	Holden	5/-
Xenophon	Agesilaus	Hailstone	2/6
,,	Anabasis Vol. I. Text	Pretor	3/-
,,	,, Vol. II. Notes	,,	4/6
,,	,, I, II	,,	4/-
,,	,, I, III, IV, V	,,	2/- each
,,	,, II, VI, VII	,,	2/6 each
† ,,	,, I, II, III, IV, V, VI	Edwards	1/6 each
	(*With complete Vocabularies*)		
,,	Hellenics I, II	,,	3/6
,,	Cyropaedeia I	Shuckburgh	2/6
,,	,, II	,,	2/-
,,	,, III, IV, V	Holden	5/-
,,	,, VI, VII, VIII	,,	5/-
,,	Memorabilia I	Edwards	2/6
,,	,, II	,,	2/6

LATIN.

Author	Work	Editor	Price
Bede	Eccl. History III, IV	Lumby	7/6
Caesar	De Bello Gallico		
	Com. I, III, VI, VIII	Peskett	1/6 each
,,	,, II–III, and VII	,,	2/- each
,,	,, I–III	,,	3/-
,,	,, IV–V	,,	1/6
† ,,	,, I, II, III, IV, V, VI, VII	Shuckburgh	1/6 each
	(*With complete Vocabularies*)		
,,	De Bello Civili. Com. I	Peskett	3/-
,,	,, ,, Com. III	,,	2/6
Cicero	Actio Prima in C. Verrem	Cowie	1/6
,,	De Amicitia	Reid	3/6
,,	De Senectute	,,	3/6
,,	De Officiis. Bk III	Holden	2/-
,,	Pro Lege Manilia	Nicol	1/6
,,	Div. in Q. Caec. et Actio Prima in C. Verrem	Heitland & Cowie	3/-
,,	Ep. ad Atticum. Lib. II	Pretor	3/-
,,	Orations against Catiline	Nicol	2/6
† ,,	In Catilinam I	Flather	1/6
	(*With Vocabulary*)		
,,	Philippica Secunda	Peskett	3/6
,,	Pro Archia Poeta	Reid	2/-

THE PITT PRESS SERIES, ETC.

LATIN continued.

Author	Work	Editor	Price
Cicero	Pro Balbo	Reid	1/6
,,	,, Milone	,,	2/6
,,	,, Murena	Heitland	3/-
,,	,, Plancio	Holden	4/6
,,	,, Sulla	Reid	3/6
,,	Somnium Scipionis	Pearman	2/-
Cornelius Nepos	Four parts	Shuckburgh	1/6 each
Erasmus	Colloquia Latina	G. M. Edwards	1/6
Horace	Epistles. Bk I	Shuckburgh	2/6
,,	Odes and Epodes	Gow	5/-
,,	Odes. Books I, III	,,	2/- each
,,	,, Books II, IV; Epodes	,,	1/6 each
,,	Satires. Book I	,,	2/-
Juvenal	Satires	Duff	5/-
Livy	Book I	H. J. Edwards	In the Press
,,	,, II	Conway	2/6
,,	,, IV, IX, XXVII	Stephenson	2/6 each
,,	,, VI	Marshall	2/6
,,	,, V	Whibley	2/6
,,	,, XXI, XXII	Dimsdale	2/6 each
,, (adapted from)	Story of the Kings of Rome	G. M. Edwards	1/6
,, ,,	Horatius and other Stories	,,	1/6
Lucan	Pharsalia. Bk I	Heitland & Haskins	1/6
,,	De Bello Civili. Bk VII	Postgate	2/-
Lucretius	Book III	Duff	2/-
,,	,, V	,,	2/-
Ovid	Fasti. Book VI	Sidgwick	1/6
,,	Metamorphoses, Bk I	Dowdall	1/6
,,	,, Bk VIII	Summers	1/6
†,,	Selections from the Tristia (*With Vocabulary*)	Simpson	1/6
†Phaedrus	Fables. Bks I and II (*With Vocabulary*)	Flather	1/6
Plautus	Epidicus	Gray	3/-
,,	Stichus	Fennell	2/6
,,	Trinummus	Gray	3/6
Pliny	Letters. Book VI	Duff	2/6
Quintus Curtius	Alexander in India	Heitland & Raven	3/6
Sallust	Catiline	Summers	2/-
,,	Jugurtha	,,	2/6
Tacitus	Agricola and Germania	Stephenson	3/-
,,	Hist. Bk I	Davies	2/6
,,	,, Bk III	Summers	2/6
Terence	Hautontimorumenos	Gray	3/-
Vergil	Aeneid I to XII	Sidgwick	1/6 each
† ,,	I, II, V, VI, IX, X, XI, XII (*With complete Vocabularies*)	,,	1/6 each
,,	Bucolics	,,	1/6
,,	Georgics I, II, and III, IV	,,	2/- each
,,	Complete Works, Vol. I, Text	,,	3/6
,,	,, ,, Vol. II, Notes	,,	4/6

THE PITT PRESS SERIES, ETC.

FRENCH.

*The Volumes marked * contain Vocabulary.*

Author	Work	Editor	Price
About	Le Roi des Montagnes	Ropes	2/-
*Biart	Quand j'étais petit, Pts I, II	Boïelle	2/- *each*
Boileau	L'Art Poétique	Nichol Smith	2/6
Corneille	La Suite du Menteur	Masson	2/-
,,	Polyeucte	Braunholtz	2/-
,,	Le Cid	Eve	2/-
De Bonnechose	Lazare Hoche	Colbeck	2/-
,,	Bertrand du Guesclin	Leathes	2/-
* ,,	,, Part II	,,	1/6
Delavigne	Louis XI	Eve	2/-
,,	Les Enfants d'Edouard	,,	2/-
De Lamartine	Jeanne d'Arc	Clapin & Ropes	1/6
De Vigny	La Canne de Jonc	Eve	1/6
*Dumas	La Fortune de D'Artagnan	Ropes	2/-
*Enault	Le Chien du Capitaine	Verrall	2/-
Erckmann-Chatrian	La Guerre	Clapin	3/-
,,	Waterloo	Ropes	3/-
,,	Le Blocus	,,	3/-
,,	Madame Thérèse	,,	3/-
,,	Histoire d'un Conscrit	,,	3/-
Gautier	Voyage en Italie (Selections)	Payen Payne	3/-
Guizot	Discours sur l'Histoire de la Révolution d'Angleterre	Eve	2/6
Hugo	Les Burgraves	,,	2/6
*Malot	Remi et ses Amis	Verrall	2/-
* ,,	Remi en Angleterre	,,	2/-
Merimée	Colomba (*Abridged*)	Ropes	2/-
Michelet	Louis XI & Charles the Bold	,,	2/6
Molière	Le Bourgeois Gentilhomme	Clapin	1/6
,,	L'École des Femmes	Saintsbury	2/6
,,	Les Précieuses ridicules	Braunholtz	2/-
,,	,, (*Abridged Edition*)	,,	1/-
,,	Le Misanthrope	,,	2/6
,,	L'Avare	,,	2/6
*Perrault	Fairy Tales	Rippmann	1/6
Piron	La Métromanie	Masson	2/-
Ponsard	Charlotte Corday	Ropes	2/-
Racine	Les Plaideurs	Braunholtz	2/-
,,	,, (*Abridged Edition*)	,,	1/-
,,	Athalie	Eve	2/-
Saintine	Picciola	Ropes	2/-
Sandeau	Mdlle de la Seiglière	,,	2/-
Scribe & Legouvé	Bataille de Dames	Bull	2/-
Scribe	Le Verre d'Eau	Colbeck	2/-
Sédaine	Le Philosophe sans le savoir	Bull	2/-
Souvestre	Un Philosophe sous les Toits	Eve	2/-
,,	Le Serf & Le Chevrier de Lorraine	Ropes	2/-

THE PITT PRESS SERIES, ETC.

FRENCH continued.

Author	Work	Editor	Price
*Souvestre	Le Serf	Ropes	1/6
Spencer	A Primer of French Verse		3/-
Staël, Mme de	Le Directoire	Masson & Prothero	2/-
,,	Dix Années d'Exil (Book II chapters 1—8)	,,	2/-
Thierry	Lettres sur l'histoire de France (XIII—XXIV)	,,	2/6
,,	Récits des Temps Mérovingiens, I—III	Masson & Ropes	3/-
Villemain	Lascaris ou les Grecs du XVe Siècle	Masson	2/-
Voltaire	Histoire du Siècle de Louis XIV, in three parts	Masson & Prothero	2/6 each
Xavier de Maistre	La Jeune Sibérienne. Le Lépreux de la Cité d'Aoste	Masson	1/6

GERMAN.

*The Volumes marked * contain Vocabulary.*

*Andersen	Eight Fairy Tales	Rippmann	2/6
Benedix	Dr Wespe	Breul	3/-
Freytag	Der Staat Friedrichs des Grossen	Wagner	2/-
,,	Die Journalisten	Eve	2/6
Goethe	Knabenjahre (1749—1761)	Wagner & Cartmell	2/-
,,	Hermann und Dorothea	,, ,,	3/6
,,	Iphigenie	Breul	3/6
*Grimm	Selected Tales	Rippmann	3/-
Gutzkow	Zopf und Schwert	Wolstenholme	3/6
Hackländer	Der geheime Agent	E. L. Milner Barry	3/-
Hauff	Das Bild des Kaisers	Breul	3/-
,,	Das Wirthshaus im Spessart	Schlottmann & Cartmell	3/-
*,,	Die Karavane	Schlottmann	3/-
*,,	Der Scheik von Alessandria	Rippmann	2/6
Immermann	Der Oberhof	Wagner	3/-
*Klee	Die deutschen Heldensagen	Wolstenholme	3/-
Kohlrausch	Das Jahr 1813	Cartmell	2/-
Lessing	Minna von Barnhelm	Wolstenholme	3/-
Lessing & Gellert	Selected Fables	Breul	3/-
Mendelssohn	Selected Letters	Sime	3/-
Raumer	Der erste Kreuzzug	Wagner	2/-
Riehl	Culturgeschichtliche Novellen	Wolstenholme	3/-
*,,	Die Ganerben & Die Gerechtigkeit Gottes	,,	3/-
Schiller	Wilhelm Tell	Breul	2/6
,,	(Abridged Edition)	,,	1/6

THE PITT PRESS SERIES, ETC.

GERMAN *continued.*

Author	Work	Editor	Price
Schiller	Geschichte des dreissigjährigen Kriegs. Book III.	Breul	3/-
,,	Maria Stuart	,,	3/6
,,	Wallenstein I. (Lager and Piccolomini)	,,	3/6
,,	Wallenstein II. (Tod)	,,	3/6
Sybel	Prinz Eugen von Savoyen	Quiggin	2/6
Uhland	Ernst, Herzog von Schwaben	Wolstenholme	3/6
	Ballads on German History	Wagner	2/-
	German Dactylic Poetry	,,	3/-

SPANISH.

Le Sage & Isla	Los Ladrones de Asturias	Kirkpatrick	3/-
Galdós	Trafalgar	,,	4/-

ENGLISH.

Bacon	History of the Reign of King Henry VII	Lumby	3/-
,,	Essays	West	3/6 & 5/-
,,	New Atlantis	G. C. M. Smith	1/6
Burke	American Speeches	Innes	3/-
Cowley	Essays	Lumby	4/-
Defoe	Robinson Crusoe, Part I	Masterman	2/-
Earle	Microcosmography	West	3/- & 4/-
Goldsmith	Traveller and Deserted Village	Murison	1/6
Gray	Poems	Tovey	4/- & 5/-
† ,,	Ode on the Spring and The Bard	,,	8*d.*
† ,,	Ode on the Spring and The Elegy	,,	8*d.*
Kingsley	The Heroes	E. A. Gardner	2/-
Lamb	Tales from Shakespeare. 2 Series	Flather	1/6 each
Macaulay	Lord Clive	Innes	1/6
,,	Warren Hastings	,,	1/6
,,	William Pitt and Earl of Chatham	,,	2/6
† ,,	John Bunyan	,,	1/-
† ,,	John Milton	Flather	1/6
,,	Lays and other Poems	,,	1/6
Mayor	A Sketch of Ancient Philosophy from Thales to Cicero		3/6
,,	Handbook of English Metre		2/-
More	History of King Richard III	Lumby	3/6
,,	Utopia	,,	3/6
Milton	Arcades	Verity	1/6
,,	Ode on the Nativity, L'Allegro, Il Penseroso & Lycidas	,,	2/6
† ,,	Comus & Lycidas	,,	2/-
,,	Samson Agonistes	,,	2/6
,,	Sonnets	,,	1/6
,,	Paradise Lost, six parts	,,	2/- *each*
Pope	Essay on Criticism	West	2/-

THE PITT PRESS SERIES, ETC.

ENGLISH *continued.*

Author	Work	Editor	Price
Scott	Marmion	Masterman	2/6
,,	Lady of the Lake	,,	2/6
,,	Lay of the last Minstrel	Flather	2/-
,,	Legend of Montrose	Simpson	2/6
,,	Lord of the Isles	Flather	2/-
,,	Old Mortality	Nicklin	2/6
,,	Kenilworth	Flather	2/6
,,	The Talisman	A. S. Gaye	2/-
Shakespeare	A Midsummer-Night's Dream	Verity	1/6
,,	Twelfth Night	,,	1/6
,,	Julius Caesar	,,	1/6
,,	The Tempest	,,	1/6
,,	King Lear	,,	1/6
,,	Merchant of Venice	,,	1/6
,,	King Richard II	,,	1/6
,,	As You Like It	,,	1/6
,,	King Henry V	,,	1/6
,,	Macbeth	,,	1/6
Shakespeare & Fletcher	Two Noble Kinsmen	Skeat	3/6
Sidney	An Apologie for Poetrie	Shuckburgh	3/-
Wallace	Outlines of the Philosophy of Aristotle		4/6
West	Elements of English Grammar		2/6
,,	English Grammar for Beginners		1/-
,,	Key to English Grammars		3/6 *net*
Carlos	Short History of British India		1/-
Mill	Elementary Commercial Geography		1/6
Bartholomew	Atlas of Commercial Geography		3/-
Robinson	Church Catechism Explained		2/-
Jackson	The Prayer Book Explained. Part I		2/6
,,	,, Part II *In preparation*		

MATHEMATICS.

Author	Work	Editor	Price
Ball	Elementary Algebra		4/6
†Blythe	Geometrical Drawing		
	Part I		2/6
	Part II		2/-
Euclid	Books I—VI, XI, XII	Taylor	5/-
,,	Books I—VI	,,	4/-
,,	Books I—IV	,,	3/-
	Also separately		
,,	Books I, & II; III, & IV; V, & VI; XI, & XII		1/6 *each*
,,	Solutions to Exercises in Taylor's Euclid	W. W. Taylor	10/6
	And separately		
,,	Solutions to Bks I—IV	,,	6/-
,,	Solutions to Books VI. XI	,,	6/-

THE PITT PRESS SERIES, ETC.

MATHEMATICS *continued*.

Author	Work	Editor	Price
Hobson & Jessop	Elementary Plane Trigonometry		4/6
Loney	Elements of Statics and Dynamics		7/6
	Part I. Elements of Statics		4/6
,,	II. Elements of Dynamics		3/6
,,	Elements of Hydrostatics		4/6
,,	Solutions to Examples, Hydrostatics		5/-
,,	Solutions of Examples, Statics and Dynamics		7/6
,,	Mechanics and Hydrostatics		4/6
†Sanderson	Geometry for Young Beginners		1/4
Smith, C.	Arithmetic for Schools, with or without answers		3/6
,,	Part I. Chapters I—VIII. Elementary, with or without answers		2/-
,,	Part II. Chapters IX—XX, with or without answers		2/-
Hale, G.	Key to Smith's Arithmetic		7/6

EDUCATIONAL SCIENCE.

†Bidder & Baddeley	Domestic Economy		4/6
†Bosanquet	{ The Education of the Young from the *Republic* of Plato }		2/6
†Burnet	Aristotle on Education		2/6
Comenius	Life and Educational Works	S. S. Laurie	3/6
	Three Lectures on the Practice of Education:		
Eve	I. On Marking	}	
Sidgwick	II. On Stimulus	} 1 vol.	2/-
Abbott	III. On the Teaching of Latin Verse Composition	}	
Farrar	General Aims of the Teacher	} 1 vol.	1/6
Poole	Form Management	}	
†Hope & Browne	A Manual of School Hygiene		3/6
Locke	Thoughts on Education	R. H. Quick	3/6
†MacCunn	The Making of Character		2/6
Milton	Tractate on Education	O. Browning	2/-
Sidgwick	On Stimulus		1/-
Thring	Theory and Practice of Teaching		4/6

†Shuckburgh	A Short History of the Greeks	4/6
†Woodward	A Short History of the Expansion of the British Empire (1500—1902)	4/-
† ,,	An Outline History of the British Empire (1500—1902)	1/6 *net*

CAMBRIDGE UNIVERSITY PRESS WAREHOUSE,
C. F. CLAY, Manager.
London: FETTER LANE, E.C.
Glasgow: 50, WELLINGTON STREET.

Milton Keynes UK
Ingram Content Group UK Ltd.
UKHW051023250324
439991UK00008B/995